THEADMAN

"ASK FOR AND EXPECT *Great*
IMMEDIATE RESULTS"

JIM MUDD AND CLIFTON LAMBRETH

D0369438

Dedication

In telling this story, I am thinking of those who helped to make it possible. It can be narrowed to three specific areas of life that have strengthened me on this journey: faith, family and friends.

It was July 1, 1981, when it started. Cecelia and our daughter, Mary Kay, had prepared an office for me in the basement of our house. It consisted of a desk and chair from a garage sale and a telephone. As I approached the desk that first morning, I remember kneeling down beside it and asking for strength and grace from the Father and His Son, Jesus Christ. My prayer was that He would show me and guide me in all things pertaining to the growth of this business; to partner with me, if you will. Don Hunt, co-founder of Hunt Brothers Pizza, out of Nashville, Tennessee, made a special trip to Cedar Falls to introduce Jesus Christ in a new and different way. Were it not for that special introduction and intervention, none of this story could have happened. Understanding in my heart the love of Jesus Christ was wonderful and sustaining. Not only were my prayers answered, but He inspired my wife,

Cecelia, and the five youngsters we had at the time. Without the love and encouragement and sacrifice that Cecelia provided during the low and scary times, I may have given up. There were many days when I was gone from home and she was there alone raising our family. Family is important in our success. Because of her teaching and showing the value of hard work and faith to the kids, one day they would bring their special talents to the business. When Kathleen was born, she is our sixth, we knew that she was a special gift from God - she was a sign that all was well with us.

As for friends, there are too many to mention them by name, but a few will never be forgotten. The Deery family in Cedar Falls, Iowa, offered their support and taught me most of what I know about the automobile business. It was from their confidence in me that kept me going from dealership to dealership to help me understand the principles you'll read about in this book. It was Ray Green of Springfield, Illinois, a friend from my radio days, who really jump started Mudd Advertising when he encouraged NADA to invite me to do the advertising workshop in 1986 at their annual convention in New Orleans. Wow, what a boost that was. It was the springboard into the national dealer body. I spoke many times after that at NADA conventions in San Francisco, Las Vegas, Atlanta and Orlando. We met and started doing business with Brooks Hanna in 1986. He has been a strong positive influence that has helped us build up others. He reminds us to get rid of, as he calls it, "stinkin' thinkin'." He has been a loyal customer and friend for many years. Of course, there were many competitors, too! One competitor was Competitive Edge led by Lee Galles, who, in my mind, was the "godfather" of automotive advertising as we know it today. I admired him so much, I read and reread his books and attended his seminars to get a grasp on how to guide dealers through the maze of advertising and media advice they were getting from everyone they knew. It was during the last years of his life that we became close friends. He visited our facilities and we his - he was a wonder to us.

Faith has played a key role in my personal and professional life. My religious faith has provided me with strength and guidance throughout my life. The faith my wife has always had in me starting and managing the business has been in-valuable. The faith that our clients have provided in our company delivering results for their businesses has been key to our business strategy. The faith I have in my family to continue to grow our business by providing excellent service to our clients provides me with peace of mind. I have faith in America and the free enterprise system to provide opportunities to everyone. I am proud and thankful for my faith.

We give our thanks to God for the many wonderful people throughout our lives – our friends and families, clients, vendors, and the great people who have worked at our company throughout the years. We are excited about what the future holds and the continuous learning and new friends that will join us along the way!

Acknowledgements

It is our sincere hope that this book can change the lives of our employees, our clients and friends, both new and old. We are so appreciative to all of those who had a part in making this book happen. It has been a fun experience, but we couldn't have done it alone.

Our thanks to Lauren Ernest, Natalie Thostenson, Aaron Sweeny, and Kyle McDowell for the creative illustrations, icons and cover design. They put in a lot of effort with quick turnarounds and some late nights to get to where we are at press time.

We are grateful to those who helped edit the book. Heather Wirtz edited much of the book in the beginning and will coordinate and direct the marketing team's campaign for the book's release. Rich and Bonnie Hoewing spent many hours editing the entire book and many versions up to press time. Wendy Jermier reworked chapter five multiple times as well as editing the rest of the book. Jackie Albrecht assisted in editing and worked on the endorsements for the book.

Special thanks to Jed Smith as he gave us the start for and helped create chapter five with his notes from Dan Gable's presentation to the UNI football team. From his notes, Jed created two training sessions for Mudd Advertising that inspired chapter five.

We appreciate the work of Chris and Rick Vernon and their team getting the "S" ring and pin information and opportunity for our book and readers.

We are truly grateful for all the direction and great advice shared with us throughout this process. Jim Mudd Jr. was the initial driver and kept the direction going to get the book to its press day. Rob Mudd added his ideas and renamed the chapters of the book for us. Chris Mudd and Mark Rolinger provided great advice to have chapter 5 reworked. Don Hunt helped immensely with the dedication and to get the book to where it is. We are thankful for Ken Blanchard's advice, direction and the great foreword he wrote for us. Dr. Chris Edgington and Jo Dorrance shared publishing information and ideas. From advice Dr. Bill

Allyson gave on an early version of the book, changes were made to get us on the right track. Dr. Bill Withers gave us his continuous support and has helped with company training.

We appreciate the work of Jacky McGrane throughout this journey. Jacky coordinated the many details that are involved from the onset through publishing, such as getting the manuscripts out, following up on them and providing editing assistance. We owe a special debt of gratitude to Jim Sartorius. Jim has been with Mudd Advertising over 20 years and introduced me to Ken Blanchard. Jim was involved with this book from the start and has been indispensable throughout the whole process. He spent many hours editing, making calls, coordinating with printers, verifying details and kept us all on task. We honestly could not have done this project without his tireless enthusiasm.

Believe you can, and you can. Belief is one of the most powerful of all problem dissolvers. When you believe that a difficulty can be overcome, you are more than halfway to victory over it already.

NORMAN VINCENT PEALE

Foreword

When I sat down and read *The Ad Man,* it put a smile on my face for two reasons.

First of all, although it is a fictionalized story, I knew it was about the amazing journey that Jim Mudd has been on for decades to create, from scratch, one of the premier advertising agencies in the automotive field. It's a story not just about Jim, but about his wife, his kids, and the ups and downs and joys and challenges of creating a great family business and learning culture. *The Ad Man* is not just about business, it's about life and how learning is truly a never-ending process.

The second reason I smiled is that I had just finished a book co-authored with Mark Miller, the vice president of training and development for Chick-fil-A, entitled *Great Leaders GROW*.   It's essentially about becoming a leader for life.   **GROW** is an acronym for what people must do to be a great leader.   I don't know two leaders who model what Mark and I are teaching more than Jim Mudd and Clifton Lambreth.   They both are looking constantly for ways to grow, and you will see good examples of this philosophy throughout *The Ad Man*.

G stands for gain knowledge.   To be a great leader, you need to continue to gain knowledge about yourself, the people around you, your industry, and leadership.   The central character in this book is continually looking for new ways to gain knowledge.   **R** stands for reach out to others by looking for "teachable moments."   You will never become a great leader if you hoard what you have learned and don't share it with others, both formally and informally, in your organization. When Jim or Clifton learn something new, they are eager to share it with others.

O suggests that if you want to be a great leader, you need to open your world to new opportunities to learn at work as well as outside of work. And finally, **W** suggests that great leaders walk toward wisdom. They are always open to feedback and self-evaluation as well as counsel from others who might mentor them. I don't know two people who open their world or walk toward wisdom more than Jim and Clifton.

I know that *The Ad Man* will not only be a good read, it will also help you on your journey to be a great leader. Enjoy and apply what you learn.

Ken Blanchard

Coauthor of *The One Minute Manager*®

17

Notes:_____

_____
_____
_____
_____
_____
_____
_____
_____
_____
_____
_____
_____
_____
_____
_____
_____
_____
_____
_____
_____
_____
_____
_____
_____
_____
_____
_____
_____
_____
_____
_____
_____
_____
_____
_____
_____

Goals:_____

66 All successful people have a goal. No one can get anywhere unless he knows where he wants to be and what he wants to do or be. 99

NORMAN VINCENT PEALE

Introduction

The Ad Man provides a story of an individual who has experienced setbacks and failure but persists until he succeeds. Faced with devastating adversity, Jim is forced to re-invent himself in a new industry. He learns to develop new skills to move from barely surviving to thriving in a changing world.

After losing his business and worrying he cannot support his wife and five young children, Jim encounters an old friend and former client who offers to set up a mentoring program to help Jim transition into a new industry. Jim begins a journey where he learns several key time tested principles that have helped others to reach their full potential.

Follow along with Jim as he visits different automobile dealers across the country to discover skills and philosophies that have made them leaders in their communities and their industry. These lessons are universal truths that can help any individual who is attempting to perform at a higher level in their industry. As Jim is filled with a desire to turn his life around, learn as he did what it takes to be successful in business and life.

The Ad Man also gives long overdue credit to a group of incredible entrepreneurs that are often overlooked – American automotive dealers. Each day, they manage complex businesses and provide millions of jobs and local community support across America. They are part of the framework of every community in which they are located through their generous support of local charities, arts, civic group, sports and entertainment.

Each of the vehicles they sell is made up of over 15,000 parts providing millions of production jobs. The assembly of these vehicles is made possible by the sales and marketing efforts of the American automobile dealers.

The authors of The Ad Man wish to acknowledge and thank the automotive dealers for their part in the development of America through their efforts to meet the transportation needs of the communities in which they operate.

Enjoy Jim's wild ride to find out what really matters in life!

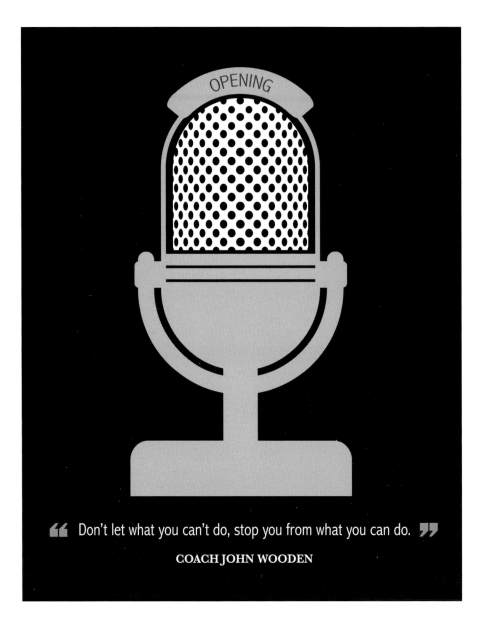

Don't let what you can't do, stop you from what you can do.

COACH JOHN WOODEN

Opening

"There is in the worst of fortune the best of chances for a happy change."

Euripides

Jim could hardly believe what had transpired today. He had lost a true friend, well maybe not a friend, but a business he had owned for many years and had counted on retiring with. For the last 25 years, Jim had been in the radio broadcast business but now, there would not be a 26th year. He had just sold his business but it did not end quite like he expected. Times had been hard of late. In fact, the last year and a half, including the last 90 days of getting FCC approval to sell the station, had been a real struggle to keep the station going. His wife and family had pitched in and did a lot of the work as they all realized the station was in dire straits. The trials of the last year and a half had helped bring their family together as they fought valiantly to keep the station going, but it was not enough as they were now at a point that they needed to sell the station. He had always thought that when someone sells a business, they leave with a big check. That was the way he had heard the story goes, but this story had a different ending. While he had been successful for some time, the market had changed and he had to let the business go to pay its debts. He signed all the papers and the new owners took over the business but no check, just a friendly good-bye handshake. He had enjoyed his career as a radio broadcaster and part owner of a station, but that was gone now. He was left to wonder what his next career steps would be.

As he returned home, he prepared himself to let his wife and family know that their struggle had come to an end and now he was without a job and career but that they were alive, healthy, and all had each other. He was not sure what was next but he knew he had five kids to put through school and his wife to support. Right now, he thought he should take some time to get it sorted out in his own mind first. It had all happened so fast. Jim had always heard "everything happens for a reason" but why, he wondered?

As he entered his home, the phone rang. It was for him. Not knowing who it was or what it was about, he took the call in the back room. Maybe he had not signed something right at the business closing or maybe there was more paperwork to do to complete the sale. Cautiously, he said, "Hello."

At the other end of the line was a friendly, comforting voice. "Hi, this is John, your old buddy." What a relief, it was an old client and friend who wanted to have dinner with him to discuss some business deals he thought Jim might be interested in. "I would love to meet you tomorrow for dinner. 7:00 PM at the diner sounds great!" He almost felt like he was imagining the conversation – it seemed so surreal. As he hung up the phone, he still wondered how he was going to explain everything to his wife and how he was going to provide for his family in the future.

Jim had an uneasy feeling in his stomach. It had literally been decades since he contemplated a career change. His mind was racing as to what he needed to do or who he should call. The situation seemed almost overwhelming at the moment. But then, he thought back to the days, right out of college, when he sold cigarettes and cigars on the streets of Owensboro to make ends meet. He also remembered selling pizzas to help get by while he was waiting to sell the radio station. He got through all that so he could surely get through this challenge, but he still wondered how. He tried to reassure himself that everything would be okay, but he still had many doubts.

He felt like one of those characters in a movie who finds himself with the devil on one shoulder barking out negative direction and breeding concern about his current situation, and the angel on the other shoulder reminding him of the positive opportunities that the future could offer. Right now, it seemed as if their arguments were just about even. While he had always believed that challenges are just opportunities to test your faith and excel, fear had begun to creep in. The tug of war between these two on his shoulder was draining most of his energy.

"It takes as much courage to have tried and failed as it does to have tried and succeeded."

ANNE MORROW LINDBERGH

Chapter 1

Get Back Up

"It's hard to beat a person

that never gives up."

Babe Ruth

Jim arrived at the restaurant early to gather his thoughts. He wondered how he would break the news to his friend that he and his partners had sold the radio station and he was not sure what he was going to be doing in the future. He had enjoyed working with this client and they had become good friends. This client had always challenged him to go further and be more creative. It was his favorite account at the radio station.

His friend, John, was a successful automobile dealer and the biggest client of his former radio station. John was just walking in when Jim spotted him at the front counter. John waved and then he began heading back toward Jim's booth. However, his friend took quite awhile to get there. Along the way, he spoke to every waitress, the owner, several customers, and even stopped to have a conversation with the busboy who was working there. It seemed John knew everyone in town or at least in this restaurant. To Jim, who was nervously awaiting John, and still not sure what he would tell him about the radio station, it seemed like it took him 30 minutes to get to the booth. John finally arrived, shook hands with Jim and was seated. John started with small talk about Jim's family and his own.

Jim was watching John, trying to figure out if he knew about the sale of the radio station or not, but he didn't dare say anything yet. After a few minutes of small talk, John told Jim that he had been watching him for several years and that his radio campaigns and marketing ideas were the best he had ever heard. His retail mind set made them different from all the others John had been pitched before. They also worked twice as well as the other approaches he had tried over the years with his business. "Jim," John said, "You are a true original. They are hard to find but easy to recognize and that is why I wanted to talk to you about taking over running all of my advertising accounts. You are the best Ad Man I have ever worked with." While he knew that John had been happy with his work, Jim could hardly believe his ears. It sounded like John wanted to hire him! Jim listened intently, cautiously optimistic.

John proceeded to share with him many of the details of running a successful car dealership that he was struggling with. There were so many different departments: new car sales, parts, service, used cars, finance and insurance, etc. On top of that, there are personnel issues to deal with as the business has grown. "Well," John said, "There just isn't enough time to manage our advertising campaigns effectively. I know how critical these are to my dealership's continued success and there is no one I can trust like you to run this part of the business. Would you consider this?"

Jim sat there in stunned silence for a few minutes. He was not sure how to respond – it seemed like an answer to his prayers. He asked John to tell him more about what he wanted Jim to do, while he attempted to gather his thoughts about this apparent offer of some kind. John continued, "I know you aren't an advertising company or agent but I bet if you tried, you could become the best one. And, I would be honored to be your first client."

Jim found himself almost in tears over this potential offer – it truly felt like an answer to his prayer. The past 24 hours had been an emotional rollercoaster. After graciously accepting John's offer, he began to share with him what had happened the previous day and how he was transitioning from the radio business. John just smiled and said, "Then the timing is perfect. You know what they say when you can't change the direction of the wind, then you adjust your sails!" They both smiled. Jim thought to himself, "Maybe things do happen for a reason after all, at just the right time."

Jim agreed to do whatever it took to make his new advertising business succeed. John reminded him to keep a positive attitude and shared that he believed too many people were opening their umbrellas prematurely before it ever began to rain. They were going through life expecting the worst and weren't surprised when they got it! He said he who expects nothing would never be disappointed.

John shared with Jim that quite a few years back when he was facing difficult times – with interest rates in double digits and gas prices at an all time high, his friends reminded him of some key principles that never fail to help generate results in difficult times. They also shared their views that if John's "yesterdays" still look big, that meant he wasn't doing enough today. He had learned that many times what we take for granted today seemed nearly impossible yesterday. Finally, they had taught him that while there were many ways to become a failure, never taking a chance is one of the best. John seemed particularly reflective as he said he had never forgotten these lessons.

Jim was already feeling this was quite a memorable day and that he would not be likely to forget these either. John shared that he believed a person was never fulfilled until they were serving others by doing what they ought to be doing. He believed that Jim was "the Ad Man" and should be running his own advertising agency. John then said, "I see promise in your future as an Ad Man and, as a coach of mine once shared with me, "Success is never final and failure is never fatal, it is the courage to continue that counts."

Now, John shifted gears back to the present opportunity. He got very serious and said, "Jim, there are some conditions we must discuss first. I have some friends I would like you to meet to provide some guidance for you and your advertising agency. When I first took over the dealership, they helped me develop my leadership skills and mentored me. I would say 90% of my success is because of them and their principles. I owe all that I have and all that I have become to these principles and my friends' guidance."

John then suggested that Jim take notes on the key principles and ideas shared on each visit. He also suggested that Jim follow a very precise strategy for taking notes and learning to maximize his retention. He believed this would be helpful in increasing his learning accuracy when it came time to process these principles in his own company and should be useful if or when he chose to share them in the future. He suggested as they share a principle to immediately write it down to allow his brain to process every principle quickly and that focus of trying to write everything down would help prevent his mind from wandering. He then suggested that Jim should ask the speaker any questions that may arise so he would make sure he fully understood what had been shared. He also suggested that he read his notes several times before going to bed and rewrite them if necessary to keep them organized. He thought this was a great strategy for learning and would have come in handy when he was in college. John recommended that in addition to taking notes on the principles he was going to learn, that whatever ideas their thoughts caused him to think of, he should write them down also.

"With your creativity and their coaching, the sky is the limit!" John concluded. He thanked John and agreed to meet with whomever he believed could help. He was excited about helping his friend expand his business through more effective advertising.

John responded that he would have one of his friends call Jim tomorrow. John said, "I only ask that you listen and at least try to apply whatever they tell you to do. It has made me successful and I am sure it will help you too!" After a few bites of their remaining dinner, John continued, "Also, there is one requirement when we agree to mentor someone new." He proceeded to explain that requirement. Jim was so overwhelmed by the events of the last 24 hours that he didn't fully understand the requirement even after John explained it to him. But, he wasn't going to bring up any obstacles at this point; after all, he needed this job! He shook hands with John and said, "We have a deal."

As the two shook hands, he noticed a rather large ring on his friend's right hand with a capital "S" on it. Funny, he had never noticed the ring before when he was with John. John noticed him admiring the ring and smiled but did not explain it.

He returned home that night and told his wife about all that had happened; she told him he would be the best Ad Man ever if he put his mind to it. Her belief in his ability over the years had always been valued but at no time more than now! As he and his wife hugged, he realized he had agreed to John's "offer" but he wasn't even sure how much it paid or how he would get paid. He smiled and thought to himself that surely they could work that out in the near future. Right now, all he cared about was that he had a new job and it felt great!

The next day, Jim's wife was off to some yard sales to get a desk, a lamp and a chair to start this new advertising agency – in their basement, of course. Just as she left, early that morning, the phone rang for him. He answered it but did not recognize the voice who said, "I am a friend of John's and he asked me to call. Can you meet me Wednesday at 7:00 AM at my dealership?" Of course, he agreed, got the address and hung up. The dealership was about 100 miles from where he lived but the distance didn't seem to matter.   He was so excited about his new opportunity that he was ready to go wherever they asked him. Whatever it took, he was committed to learning the secrets to their success that had helped his friend John so much.

" You can get everything in life you want, if you help enough other people get what they want "

ZIG ZIGLAR

Chapter 2

Attitude

"I had the blues because I had no shoes

until upon the street,

I met a man who had no feet."

Ancient Persian Saying

He arrived at the dealership before 6:45 AM. The dealer was already there. He was waiting out front with a huge smile. It was a big store with an impressive lineup of vehicles in the front. The dealer motioned for him to follow him as he went into the store and directly upstairs to the conference room. There was an audience already waiting on them. It seemed like more than 50 people were there sitting, laughing and joking. But as soon as the dealer arrived in the room, the crowd became silent. He thought this reminded him of a military situation when an officer walked in.

The dealer took the first 10 minutes to brag on what seemed to be everyone in that room individually. Then he took his place at the front of the room and said, "Today, I have a friend joining us." He then introduced Jim as an Ad Man and a friend of the auto industry. Then, he went right back to his presentation, as if he were on a tight schedule.

The dealer began, "Today we are going to talk about one of the key principles that every successful person or business has to get right. It is having the right mental attitude." Then he went to the board and wrote, "Attitude determines altitude." The people in the room seemed to begin to take notes on cue. Jim began to take notes too. The dealer explained that as long as anyone has a positive attitude then there is the potential to become successful.

Then, the dealer wrote on the board, "Positive attitude produces positive results." Again, the audience was taking notes fiercely. He explained that there were many tools that could help them become more positive. By now, Jim found himself writing even more fiercely to keep up, taking notes as the dealer was sharing his secret formula for success.

The dealer then explained to the group that people may see a glass as half full or half empty and can be looking at the same glass. While these were both technically correct, focusing on what you don't have is a waste of energy and would only lead to more of the same, causing a negative downward spiral that can be hard to overcome.

On the other hand, the dealer suggested a different strategy. He returned to the board and wrote, "Focus on what you have!" He explained by regularly focusing on what you have, it keeps your mind from focusing on negative things and what you don't have. He explained the latest research on neuroscience and how the brain will literally burn new neural pathways from your positive thinking. Unfortunately, if you focus on the negative, it can burn negative neural pathways as well.

The dealer admitted that it might take some effort when you first start but by training your mind to focus on your positive assets, you would put yourself on the road to getting positive results. After a short time, your subconscious would be conditioned to instinctively first see all the positive aspects of any situation. Leveraging the positive would help maximize positive results and lead to greater success more quickly.

The dealer also shared his view that most people are willing to change, not because they see the light ahead that they can reach, but because they feel the heat of a bad situation! Seeing the light would be easier and allow them to change on their timetable. The Ad Man thought about his recent changes. He had experienced the "heat" of losing the radio station and the "light" of the opportunity to start his own agency with a great client in hand.

Next, the dealer went back to the whiteboard and wrote "Beware of the CAVE men." The crowd smiled and then laughed. The dealer proceeded to spell out an acronym:

C- Collectively

A- Against

V- Virtually

E- Everything

As the dealer stepped away revealing this, everyone began to laugh and images of cavemen like the acronym described seemed to be envisioned by all in the room. He then explained while everyone knew some of these CAVE people, spending too much time with them could be like drinking too much alcohol – it might distort your ability to function properly. Then he smiled and winked at them.

With that the crowd began to laugh for a little bit, but as the idea of those CAVE people negatively impacting the dealership or other situations began to sink in, a silence came over the crowd, much like the "wave" in a football game. Everyone began writing fiercely again. Jim had never thought about this concept that way, but it seemed to make sense. He had certainly experienced many negative types of people in his career – people who seemed to delight in finding all the reasons why not to do something.

While the group had been laughing, the dealer took a sip of his coffee. Jim noticed – on the dealer's right hand – the same ring that John had with a big "S" on it. He figured that they must have gone to school together or something. He thought to himself that he needed to ask John about it next time he saw him.

Once more, the dealer then went to the whiteboard and wrote, "Avoid stinking thinking" and proceeded to explain that negative thinking was called "stinking thinking" by a good friend of his. He reminded people to not allow others to dwell on stinking thinking because this could lead to results that smell. The crowd again laughed. The dealer had an amazing way of using humor to convey his points about important business topics.

The dealer reminded the group that they would never see the sunrise by looking to the West. To win in life, you must position yourself toward action and success. To see the sunrise you must be looking to the East! Then, the dealer returned to the whiteboard and pointed again to his sign, "Positive attitude gets positive results" only he wrote over the word, "attitude" and replaced it with "thinking" – leaving "Positive Thinking Gets Positive Results." The dealer then explained that getting a positive attitude and keeping one in a sometimes negative world might take some effort but it would pay long term dividends. He told them that he starts and ends every day with a positive thought or quote. He suggested that they invest some time with positive books, CD's and DVD's to help acquire and sustain their positive mental attitude. He reminded them that they only had 100% of their time and effort and they should apply as much as possible to focus on the positive.

Finally, he wrote on the board, "Readers are leaders and succeeders" and he lifted a piece of paper to reveal a poster on the wall with a Charles Swindoll quote. He began reading:

Attitude
by Charles Swindoll

The longer I live, the more I realize the impact of attitude on life.

Attitude, to me, is more important than facts. It is more important than the past, than education, than money, than circumstances, than failures, than successes, than what other people think or say or do. It is more important than appearance, giftedness, or skill. It will make or break a company ... a church ... a home.

The remarkable thing is we have a choice every day regarding the attitude we will embrace for that day. We cannot change our past. We cannot change the fact that people will act in a certain way. We cannot change the inevitable.

The only thing we can do is play on the one string we have, and that is our attitude ... I am convinced that life is 10% what happens to me, and 90% how I react to it. And so it is with you … we are in charge of our attitudes.

Next, the dealer lifted another piece of paper that revealed a second poster. While pointing to it, he shared another one of his favorite quotes.

Far better is it to dare mighty things, to win glorious triumphs, even though checkered by failure... than to rank with those poor spirits who neither enjoy nor suffer much, because they live in a gray twilight that knows not victory nor defeat.

Theodore Roosevelt

The dealer then said, "I believe you all were engineered for great things and designed for success just like these vehicles we represent! You just have to make sure there is fuel in the tank and the ignition key is turned on. A positive mental attitude will both put fuel in the tank and turn on your personal ignition switch so that you are ready to run!" He thanked everyone for their attention and concluded with, "Your focus determines your future. Focus on the positive. Only in algebra do two negatives equal a positive. In business and in life, two negatives equal a mess!"

And then he offered one more piece of advice, "The task does not bring dignity to the doer; the doer brings dignity to the task!" Everyone these days (many especially right out of school) seem to want the big office or the big title and often they are focused on all the wrong things. What is really important is what you accomplished at the end of the day. Do you want to be remembered for your title or what you did? A good friend of ours was the late Charlie Tremendous Jones – who lived this principle day in and day out his whole life. He'd get to work and get out of his car and just be walking from his car to his office and if he saw a piece of trash, he'd stop and pick it up and make sure it was disposed of. He lived the example of no task was too little and none too big. At the end of each day he would reflect and ask himself, as he was getting ready to head home for the day, "What could I do better tomorrow than I did today?" In fact, he had a sign hanging right above his doorway leading out of his office that asked that question as his reminder before he left each day. By reflecting on what he did that day and what could he improve upon each day he would remind himself that if he could improve just

1% every day – at the end of the year that's a lot of improvement. At the end of his life Charlie had reached his goal to have lived a life of continuous improvement!

What will you be remembered for?

With this, just like clockwork, everyone in the room stood up and began to give the other team members high fives, knuckle bumps and hugs like you might see at sporting events. Jim could tell that people from every department were fired up and were going to have a great day. He looked at his watch – 59 minutes exactly. What an impactful hour that had been!

Jim knew he was embarking on an exciting new journey meeting colleagues of John's like this dealer and learning the keys to success. He was impressed by the dealer's presentation and he wondered why such a simple message of "positive thinking gets positive results" wasn't used more often to motivate people in business or personal situations.

As he drove back to his home, he could hardly contain himself. He was more energized than he had been in a long time. His mind was reviewing all the lessons about positive attitude and thinking of what the dealer had shared that day. He lost track of time and before he knew it, he was walking in his home, just as the phone was ringing. He answered it quickly, still immersed in his thoughts about the day, which had been the most positive day he had experienced in a very long time.

The voice on the phone said, "I am a friend of John's. I was hoping we could spend the day together tomorrow." Jim did not even hear himself respond when the gentleman on the other end of the phone gave him the address and time. Jim got off the phone, hung up his jacket and tried to catch his breath. It had been a whirlwind of a day, of a week!

Jim had heard of this dealer before, though he was some distance away, perhaps 200 miles. He would have to check the map. The dealer had been a leader for his franchise for many years. Jim had occasionally seen his TV commercials on the network shows and knew he had a big store but since the dealer was not in his radio area, he had not paid much attention before. He did remember something about the dealer's television advertising boasting that he was the biggest truck dealer in seven states. That should be a sight to see. Jim could hardly wait to get started in the morning.

Before going to sleep Jim wanted to review his notes on what he had learned today. There was a lot to think about and apply as he studied the key points.

<u>Ad Man Notes - Key Principles:</u>

- Your attitude determines altitude – positive attitude = potential success.

- Positive attitude produces positive results.

- Focus on what you have, not what you don't have. Your focus determines your future.

- Beware of C.A.V.E. people – finding reasons why not to do something.

  C – Collectively

  A – Against

  V – Virtually

  E – Everything

- Avoid stinking thinking – or get smelly results.

- Positive ~~attitude~~ thinking gets positive results.

- Readers are leaders and succeeders.

- The task does not bring dignity to the doer; the doer brings dignity to the task.

- What's really important is what you accomplished today.

- What could I do better tomorrow than I did today?   [1% / day compounds to a lot]

- What will you be remembered for?

- Your Focus Determines Your Future.

- Am I living a life of continuous improvement?

The difference between perseverance and obstinacy is that one often comes from a strong will, and the other comes from a strong won't.

HENRY WARD BEECHER

Chapter 3

Commitment

"It was character that got us out of bed, commitment that moved us into action, and discipline that enabled us to follow through."

Zig Ziglar

He awoke early the next morning. He had an exciting day yesterday and could hardly wait to get on the road to meet another new friend and mentor. He wondered what lesson he might learn today. He found himself filled with excitement in anticipation. He also had remembered to start the day with a quote:

"It is easy to be happy when life goes by like a song, but the man worthwhile is the man with a smile when everything goes dead wrong."

Author - unknown

Jim had heard about this dealership before but had never met the dealer. So, he was doubly excited about the opportunity to visit with him. Jim had heard about some of the approaches this dealer had been using and his businesses seemed to grow faster than the competition. He had established himself as one of the leaders nationally in the retail automotive business for this type of franchise.

When he arrived at the dealership, he could see that the television advertising was right. He had never seen so many trucks. It looked like at least 10 acres of new trucks. As he was marveling at this dealer's inventory on both sides of the road, he noticed a short man in the front of a huge glass window waving to him to come over. The man then began moving toward Jim at a fast pace so Jim also picked up his speed to meet him.

The dealer greeted Jim, "Great to meet you! I am so excited that you could join me today." With that the dealer led Jim into the main dealership showroom. As they entered the room, Jim saw what looked to be over 100 people circled on the showroom floor. A giant "S" was in the center of the floor.

As the dealer entered the showroom, applause rang out. The dealer pointed to a seat in the front row for Jim and then the dealer took his place in the center of the huddled crowd of employees. He motioned for them to stop applauding, and they did just like there was an on/off switch.

Then the dealer began the meeting, "Today, we are going to discuss what should be a key ingredient in everybody's recipe for success. To be successful, you must be persistent." Then, he walked to the whiteboard at one end of the circle and wrote, "Hard work and persistence equals success." The audience and Jim began taking notes feverishly just like Jim's meeting the day before. The dealer's presentation involved discussing historical and current public figures who had been successful but only after experiencing failures and demonstrating perseverance by not giving up.

The first one he described, in great detail, was Abraham Lincoln. He unveiled a poster in the showroom that outlined the ordeals Lincoln had experienced to become President. The poster read:

Abraham Lincoln's Incredible Journey to

Become the 16th President of the United States!

Year/Event

1816 He had to work to support his family after they were forced out of their home.

1818 His mother died.

1831 Failed in business.

1832 Was defeated for Legislature.

1832 Lost job and couldn't get into law school.

1833 Declared bankruptcy, and spent the next 17 years of his life paying off the money he borrowed from friends to start his business.

1834 Was defeated for Legislature again.

1835 Was engaged to be married, but his sweetheart died and his heart was broken.

1836 Had a nervous breakdown and spent the next six months in bed.

1838 Was defeated in becoming the Speaker of the State.

1840 Was defeated in becoming Elector.

1843 Was defeated for Congress.

1846 Was defeated for Congress.

1848 Was defeated for Congress again.

1849 Was rejected for the job of Land Officer in his home state.

1854 Was defeated for Senate.

1856 Was defeated for Vice President – got less than 100 votes.

1858 Was defeated for Senate for the third time.

1860 Was elected President of the United States.

The dealer reminded his audience that Abraham Lincoln only had 18 months of formal education [equivalent of a 2nd grade education today].   Many in the audience sat wide-mouthed. While some had heard about a few of these trials, none of them knew the extent of Lincoln's failures before his election as President. The dealer, sensing their awe and surprise, asked, "Are you a little bit discouraged right now because you have tried and tried and still haven't achieved some of your dreams? If so, please don't be. Worthwhile goals and aspirations have always taken time to accomplish – but many give up before they do so. It took Abraham Lincoln 30 years to achieve his dream of becoming the President of the United States.   Although he faced countless, seemingly insurmountable obstacles or trials, he did not give up. He didn't quit. While it may seem impossible for you to overcome your current challenges or problems, remind yourself of the experiences of others who went before you and promise yourself that you will not give up."

The dealer then mentioned a long list of other people who had been successful because they were persistent and had persevered, despite obstacles or failures.

- *John Kennedy failed to make the football team at the Canterbury School. He failed Latin at Choate*

Academy. He lost the election for president of his freshman class at Harvard. Later, he also lost a bid for student council. He was elected to US House in 1946 and the Senate in 1952 and became 35th President of United States in 1960.

- *Ben Franklin was born 15th of 17 children to a poor candle maker. He only had one year of formal schooling. He taught himself four languages, plus science, finance and writing. He went on to become one of the most educated people in history. He became a famous inventor, diplomat and author.*

- *Babe Ruth is remembered as the "Homerun King." He was also the "Strikeout" champion. He struck out 1,330 times more than any other player in baseball history.*

The dealer said, "Remember, you don't drown by falling in the water but by staying in. When you fail, you just have to keep going. These guys didn't quit!" He continued with examples of other famous people:

- *Did you know in 1927 Lucille Ball was advised to try another profession because she was told she would never make it as an actress? She went on to be a star of one of the most successful TV shows of all time and later even owned her own movie and television studio.*

- *In 1962, an executive of Decca Records told the Beatles he didn't like their sound and that groups playing guitars were on their way out.*

- *Jack Canfield and Mark Victor Hansen were turned down by over 140 publishers before they found a publisher for their first <u>Chicken Soup for the Soul</u> book. The series has sold over 60 million copies.*

The dealer then asked, rhetorically, *"Quitters? I don't think so!"* He continued:

- *Donald Fisher once found himself frustrated by a large department store refusing to exchange a pair of Levis he had bought in the wrong size. The frustrations led him to go on to start The Gap, a wildly successful clothing store.*

- *Dr. Seuss' first book was rejected by 27 publishing houses. Once he finally was accepted by a publisher, he went on to publish more than 40 best-selling children's books and sold millions of copies.*

- *Sam Walton failed in business several times before finally starting and succeeding with Wal-Mart.*

- *Jay Leno once failed the employment test at the Woolworth's discount store. He later became a successful host of The Tonight Show.*

- *Fred Smith wrote a term paper for his class at Yale suggesting an overnight delivery business. The professor gave him a "C" on the term paper. He later raised and borrowed $95 million [Today that would be around 500 million] and started Federal Express.*

The dealer said, "Do you think these people were frustrated at the time of their failures or facing their obstacles? Sure, but these people didn't quit!" The dealer continued with a few more examples:

- *Ulysses Grant failed as a farmer, real estate agent, a custom's official and a store clerk. He went on to command the union armies during the Civil War and became the 18th President of the United States in 1868.*

- *Thomas Monaganham was born a poverty-stricken orphan and ashamed of his clothing as a child. In his adult life, he started Domino's Pizza and became a multi-millionaire.*

- *In order to support his family, Ray Kroc started selling paper cups to small restaurants. He bought the rights from the McDonald brothers to start a restaurant chain while selling them milkshake machines. Today, McDonalds is a multibillion dollar business and the largest food franchise in the world.*

- *In 1954, Jimmy Denny, then manager of the Grand Ole Opry, fired Elvis Presley after only one performance. He told him, "You ain't going nowhere son. You ought to go back to driving a truck." Elvis went on to become one of the most popular singers in the world.*

- *Thomas Edison tried over 2,000 experiments before he got the light bulb to work.*

- *In the 1940's, Chester Carlson invented a product and demonstrated it to over 20 corporations before a Rochester, New York, company purchased the rights to what is known as a Xerox copier today.*

The dealer said, "Throughout history, most successful people became successful because of their persistence and perseverance, regardless of challenges and obstacles facing them." He then went to the whiteboard and wrote, "Don't quit!" He asked them to look over at the sales tower door. There was a huge poster that had a poem entitled "Don't quit." He began to read it:

Don't Quit

When things go wrong, as they sometimes will,
When the road you're trudging seem all uphill,
When the funds are low and the debts are high,
And you want to smile, but you have to sigh,
When care is pressing you down a bit,
Rest, if you must, but don't you quit.

Life is queer with its twists and turns,
As every one of us sometimes learns,
And many a failure turns about,

When he might have won had he stuck it out,

Don't give up though the pace seems slow—

You may succeed with another blow.

Often the goal is nearer than,

It seems to a faint and faltering man,

Often the struggler has given up,

When he might have captured the victor's cup,

And he learned too late when the night slipped down,

How close he was to the golden crown.

Success is failure turned inside out—

The silver tint of the clouds of doubt,

And you never can tell how close you are,

It may be near when it seems so far,

So stick to the fight when you're hardest hit--

It's when things seem worst that you must not quit.

You could have heard a pin drop as he finished reading the poem.

As Jim looked around the circle at the team, he could see that the dealer's message was effectively delivered and received by everyone with enthusiasm and excitement.

The dealer then said, "Remember what A. Lou Vickery said. Four short words sum up what has lifted most successful individuals above the crowd: a little bit more. They did all that was expected of them and then did a little bit more."

The dealer concluded the meeting by saying, "I want everyone in this dealership to realize their full potential and become successful. Persistence must be an important ingredient in everyone's success formula." He finished by writing on the board again *"Quitters never win and winners never quit."* Like the last dealership he had visited, the excited employees mingled about a few minutes and then filed out.

The dealer asked Jim what happened on July 4th, 1776. Jim responded, "Why, that was the signing of the Declaration of Independence! I visited Independence Hall in Philadelphia several years ago on a family vacation." The dealer asked, "Did you get to go see Valley Forge where General Washington spent two winters with his troops outside of Philadelphia?" Jim shared that he and his family did the entire tour and watched the video and thoroughly enjoyed their visit. He also added those troops had to endure some pretty rough times during the winter months with limited resources.

The dealer agreed, and then he shared what most people don't think about is that those tough times were two years after 1776, the date of our supposed independence. He said, "In fact, the Continental Army still had to fight the British Army for our independence for almost two more years and over 2,000 men lost their lives at Valley Forge.

We celebrate Independence on July 4th, 1776, and the battle was just beginning then." "Jim," he said, "Even if you declare your independence, you are going to have to fight to keep it. When you start your business, it is going to be the start of a battle and don't be surprised if you have to fight to keep it longer than you thought. Just like Valley Forge, the battle did lead to freedom and eventually your perseverance can also lead your company to success."

On the drive home that night, the 200 miles flew by as his mind raced; recounting all the examples the dealer had shared with him. He was amazed to have been taught how many individuals that were famous today but would have been virtual unknowns if they had quit. He had made up his mind to be one of the winners.

His excitement about this new journey as the Ad Man was hard to contain. As he entered his home, his eyes were filled with tears. Just a few short days ago, he had lost his 25-year career, was fearful about being unemployed and felt very uncertain about the future. Now, he was confident that the journey ahead, while it might be filled with obstacles and failures, was one he would persist at and become successful. Jim wasn't sure what would happen next or where the journey would take him, but the last couple of days had filled him with hope and excitement.

Just like the previous two nights, almost like clockwork, he heard the phone ring as soon as he entered his home. He heard another friendly voice with the usual introduction, "You don't know me but I am a friend of John's. Could you meet me at 7:00 tomorrow at my dealership?" Jim agreed, the gentleman gave him the address and they hung up.

Jim had never heard of this dealer before. In fact, he wasn't sure he had even been to this town. He pulled out his atlas and looked up the town and saw that it was a small town outside of one of Iowa's major cities. This dealership was almost 150 miles away in a different direction from where he had driven today. But, by now, traveling had become no big deal and in light of the exciting meetings he had had the previous two days, he could hardly wait to get on the road again.

While Jim was excited about the opportunities of tomorrow, he knew he needed to review all his notes he had written down from today's lesson.

Ad Man Notes – Key Principles:

- Hard work and persistence equals success. – [Abe Lincoln didn't quit]

- You don't drown by falling into water but by staying in – when you fail you have to keep going.

- Many famous people would never have become famous had they not experienced setbacks and then persevered to achieve their goals regardless of the challenges and obstacles.

- Don't quit!

- Four words that have always mattered – "a little bit more."

- Quitters never win and winners never quit.

- July 4[th,] 1776 – We still had to keep fighting to keep the independence . . . keep on persevering and never ever quit.

" What's most important is that
one strives to achieve a goal. "

RONALD REAGAN

Chapter 4

Goal Setting Produces Gold

Don't bunt. Aim out of the ballpark.

David Ogilvy

Jim arrived at the next dealership early before their 7:00 AM meeting. As he pulled up, he noticed a very tall, distinguished individual standing out front and waving to Jim as he pulled up. The gentleman thanked him for coming and then explained that they had an appointment at the local county high school.

When they arrived, there was a teacher waiting to take them to the class. The teacher thanked the dealer for his commitment to their school's "Taking local business to the classroom" program and also for his support of their driver's education program for the last 10 years. The teacher shared that his two children had learned to drive in this dealer's cars and his family owned three of this dealer's vehicles. The dealer smiled at that remark and thanked the teacher for his support of the dealership for many years.

When they entered the classroom, the dealer seemed to know his way around and he took his place at the back of the room. The dealer introduced Jim as a well-known ad man and a friend of the auto industry. He then walked to the front of the class. Jim quickly pulled out his spiraled notepad and a fresh ink pen and started trying to write down everything.

The dealer wrote on the board "Your gold is in your goal setting." The dealer explained that most people never go as far as they could or as fast as they could because they don't take time to establish goals. He said, "First, it is important to set big but realistic goals. Then, it is just as important to break down your goals to a manageable level to help ensure you can measure progress toward the goal and that you don't get overwhelmed or paralyzed from getting started."

Back at the board, he next wrote, "A goal isn't a goal unless you write it down and share it with someone." He explained that the simple act of writing the goal down had been proven to increase the likelihood of goal achievement. It would help a person begin developing a plan to achieve their goals. He also said sharing a goal with someone would help keep everyone accountable for what they were trying to accomplish. He turned on the projector and showed a slide from a study by Brigham Young University, which revealed the following.

Implementing A Good Idea

- 10% of people who hear a good idea will do something about it.
- 25% will do something with it if they think (in depth) about it.
- 40% will do something with it if they prepare a plan.
- 50% will do something with it if they add times to the plan.
- 60% will do something with it if another person is asked to be involved.
- 90% will do something with it if there is a date set to follow up with the other person.

He said many people confuse their wishes with their goals. He then wrote on the board "A goal is a wish with a plan to accomplish it." He also explained that more people could do more, get more, and help more if only they set their goals higher. He then went to the board and wrote "Real goals usually took real work to accomplish them." Then, he said, "Too many people want to accomplish a goal or have a dream but don't have the will or willingness to work hard to accomplish it. Michael Jordan became an extraordinary basketball player. But, as a child, he would shoot hundreds of basketball shots every day to improve his game. It is said that Larry Bird would make at least 100 free throws every day after practice was over."

The dealer continued, "It is also important to start with big goals! Big goals take more time and more resources to accomplish. Big goals pay big dividends too! Once big goals are established, you need to write them down. It may help to start by establishing three or fewer big goals. These should be things that once they are reached will lead to significant accomplishments in your life or career. After that, you can set small goals that will take you on the road to accomplishing these big goals. Remember, small goals will need to be written down and shared with others as well. Most goals begin with a dream, a desire or a want."

He added, "It's the proximity, not the severity that makes a problem acute!" Jim wondered what the dealer meant by that? The dealer went on to explain that the problems that are the closest and may appear to be the biggest and most important are not always as big as they appear. He went on to say that once you have created your plan and set your goals – you need to stick with your plan, despite the distractions from your competitors and outside factors. "Develop your plan and work your plan. Also, you need to follow and execute the plan and when your competitor does something or other issues arise – do not knee jerk and change your whole plan or abandon everything in 'reaction mode.' This is not to say that you don't adapt on the fly, but rather use these competitive and other issues that pop up as a way to 'tweak' and fine tune your plan! Stick to your plan and your continued execution with your tweaked plan and keep running forward toward your goal! The old baseball saying about 'keeping your eye on the ball' is applicable with regards to your plan and goals . . . take the eye off yours and then focus on something else, and it will cost you the game!"

"Effective goal setting starts by looking at where you are and what you have, then determining where you want to be and what it would take to get there."

He then began writing on the board again.

You are here → you want to be there

Ask yourself: What does it take to get there?

- What do you need to learn?

- What steps can you already see that it will require?

- What or who do you need to help get you there? What resources are required to get there?

- How long could or should it take? (You should be prepared to persist for the long-term for your big goals)

- How will you know when you are there?

He also shared, "Obstacles often look bigger from far away. Once you identify them, plan for them and attack them, they seem to lose most of their size."

He then went to the board and wrote:

Obstacles are things that a person sees

when he takes his eyes off the goal.

An obstacle is an unrealized opportunity!

The dealer continued, "Even if you can find a path with no obstacles, it probably doesn't lead anywhere and you probably don't need to go there anyway." At that, the students laughed.

The dealer told the students that while it is important to stay positive, it is crucial to identify as many of the possible obstacles to accomplishing their goal as they can. He explained, "You should develop a plan to overcome them or anticipate what you will do if they occur -- and then forget about them and focus on the goal! It is also important to identify why you want to accomplish this goal. This will provide extra motivation when the going gets rough or the goal seems harder than you realized."

"It is also important to track progress toward small and big goals. Sometimes people set goals but they forget to establish how they are going to track progress toward success. This is known as the 'all-or-nothing' approach and sometimes causes individuals to become frustrated and abandon their goals or become distracted and find themselves on the wrong road away from their goals."

"You may also have to adapt your goals as conditions change. Big goals are usually not abandoned if they are realistic, you are passionate about them and there is a well-thought out plan to accomplish them. Sometimes small goals must be changed to adapt to changing business conditions or environmental changes."

As Jim listened to this dealer, he realized that having both personal and business goals is important. It struck him that, while he had achieved many successes in his career, prior to the recent downturn that led to the sale of the radio station, he had only vague goals in his mind. He had never taken the time to write down and share his goals at work or at home. For a minute or so, he even struggled to remember what some of his goals had been. Writing them down, posting them and sharing his goals would definitely have helped him.

Jim also thought that discussing big and small goals with family members or co-workers might ensure that he established the right goals. They could be important sounding boards for him, as well as accountability partners.

Tracking progress would be important to him in his new ad business. It could help him have a feeling of accomplishment and reassure him and others that progress was being made.

Jim thought how lucky these high school students were to get this message as they were preparing to take their places in college or in the working world.   He was also impressed that this dealer would take so much time to help prepare the next generation for success.

Just then he looked up and the dealer was writing on the board. "Set your goals – then crystallize your goals." The dealer explained big and small goals needed to be crystallized and that crystallized means breaking the big goals down into smaller goals and measurable action steps.

At the board, the dealer began writing an example the students could relate to:

Say your goal was to save $100 a month you:

Divide the month by 4 weeks: $25 a week
Divide by 7 days: $3.57 per day
Divide by 24 hours: 14.8 cents per hour
Divide by 60 minutes: less than a penny per minute

"Well, you get the point," the dealer explained. "While $100 a month may sound like big bucks to most of you, less than a penny a minute sounds a little easier to accomplish, doesn't it?" The class was energized and agreed. Everyone in the class could see how this process made goals more attainable.

"Crystallizing the goals makes them seem more accomplishable!" Then the dealer went back to the board and wrote. "Inch by inch – It is a cinch. Yard by yard – that is hard." He then reminded them that a way to stay motivated would be to remind themselves how they were going to use the $100 a month they were earning. He then joked that the students could consider saving to buy a vehicle at his store and the whole class began to laugh.

Last, he wrote on the board "WIFM" – what is in it for me? He explained that identifying "WIFM" provides the "why" for accomplishing their goals. He then told them that "WIFM" did not have to be self-serving. It could be that they accomplish their goals by helping others and that win/win solutions were always better than win/lose scenarios, but he added that that is a lesson for another day.

With that last point, he thanked the class for allowing him to share some of his ideas with them. The entire class rose to their feet and gave him a standing ovation. Without even being conscious of it, Jim found himself standing and clapping with the class. The dealer responded by clapping for the students as well. It was in that moment that Jim noticed the "S" ring on the dealer's right hand. This was the exact same ring that the others dealers were wearing.

There was real gratitude from both the students and the teacher for the time the dealer had shared with them. The teacher thanked the dealer for coming and sharing part of his success formula with the class.

On the way back to the dealer's car, Jim asked him how often he visited the high school. The dealer responded that it was usually a couple of times a month. Jim knew how busy the owner of a dealership was and couldn't help wonder why the dealer spent so much time helping the school. Jim decided to just ask the dealer why.   The dealer just smiled at Jim and said, "Succession planning, I guess!" At that, they both laughed as they got in the car and went back to the dealership.

The dealer said, "Remember, Jim, goals will help you steer your organization and give you a strategic approach for allocation of resources. They can also help keep the train on the right track." With this both men smiled and nodded.

On the ride home, Jim marveled about another incredible day of learning. He was learning more in a week than in years of college. Even today, which had seemed so basic and geared to students, included important lessons that many forget as they chase after their goals. It was basic, yet essential, to getting maximum performance out of life.

As if someone knew the exact time he would walk into his home from his drive, the phone once again began to ring. He quickly hurried over to the phone and answered it. Like the other three days, the voice on the other end explained that he was a friend of John's and he would be honored if Jim could meet him at his store the next morning. Jim quickly and enthusiastically answered affirmatively and hung up the phone.

This dealer was again over 100 miles away in another direction. Like the last one, it took an atlas to find it. As he looked in the atlas, he found this town right on the border of an adjoining state. By now he had grown accustomed to these drives and these meetings. But, each one was different and Jim wondered what tomorrow would bring. One thing he did feel sure of -- there would be a new and fresh lesson.

Before Jim went to bed he wanted to review and add some additional notes to the lessons he learned that day.

Ad Man Notes – Key Principles:

- Your gold is in your goal setting. A goal must be <u>written down</u> and <u>shared with someone</u> to be a true goal.

- A goal is a wish with a plan to accomplish it.

- Real goals usually take real work – Michael Jordan and Larry Bird shot hundreds of baskets after each practice ended.

- It's the proximity, not the severity that makes a problem acute – sometimes things appear

bigger and or closer than they really are – don't knee jerk and become distracted from your plan.
- Develop your plan, work your plan, and stick to your plan! Tweak the plan if you need to, but stick to your plan!

- <u>You are here → You want to be there.</u>

- Ask yourself: What does it take to get there?

- What do you need to learn?

- What steps can you already see that it will require?

- What or who do you need to help get you there? What resources are required to get there?

- How long could or should it take? (You should be prepared to persist for the long-term for your big goals.)

- How will you know when you are there?

- Obstacles are things that a person sees when he takes his eyes off the goal.

- An obstacle is an unrealized opportunity.

- Set your goals. Then, crystallize your goals by breaking big goals into smaller goals with measurable action steps. Goals need to be broken down to lowest level so progress can be tracked.

- Goals help steer the course of your actions and allocation of your resources.

- Inch by inch – It's a cinch. Yard by yard – that is hard.

- WIFM – What's In It For Me?   Provides the why for accomplishing the goals. [Not necessarily self-serving – win/win solutions and helping others.]

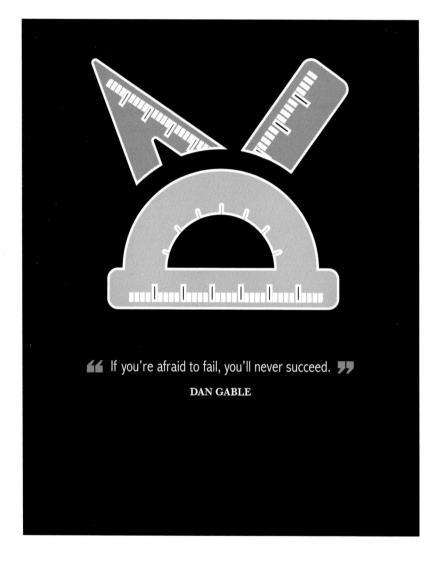

If you're afraid to fail, you'll never succeed.

DAN GABLE

Chapter 5

Measurement

"Gold medals aren't really made of gold. They're made of sweat, determination, and a hard-to-find alloy called guts."

Dan Gable

Jim was asked to arrive early at the dealership before it opened for the day. He arrived about twenty minutes ahead of schedule, just before 7:00 AM. The store was smaller than he thought it would be. Jim thought, "Maybe there are some lessons that can only be learned at smaller businesses."

He got out of his car and was immediately greeted by a very trim and cordial gentleman. "Welcome to our dealership!" He shook Jim's hand with a strong handshake.

As they head into the store, Jim notices that they probably have about six or seven sales people on the floor at this early hour and there are a handful of other staff members also gathering, probably parts and service and business office types - definitely a smaller operation though. Jim noticed each one had a smile on their face and he also noticed a different look in their eyes.

As they enter into the dealer's office, Jim notices an autographed picture on the wall and observed that one of the people in the picture looked like the famous wrestling coach, Dan Gable, shaking hands with another gentleman. As they take their seats, a man brings in a couple cups of coffee and the dealer smiles as he sees Jim looking at the picture. At the same time, two men walk into the office and Jim recognizes the first to enter the room was the other gentleman in the picture who quickly extends his hand to Jim and says, "Welcome to our store." Right behind him extending his hand is Coach Dan Gable, who adds, "Good to meet you, Jim!"

The dealer smiles as he sees Jim is surprised by meeting Dan Gable. The friend of the dealer said that he had the privilege of wrestling for Dan at the University of Iowa and he went on to say, "Once in every 500 years a man is born like Dan Gable."

His future career would lead the Iowa wrestling program to 15 national championships in 21 seasons and he is one of the most winning coaches in history with a winning percentage of .938% in Division 1. To quote one of the most winning coaches ever, Coach John Wooden said, "Dan Gable is the greatest coach of all time!"

Jim was sure this would be a great day to learn from such a successful athlete and coach.

With that, the dealer said it was 7 AM and time to address the troops as they were all gathered on the showroom floor.

They quickly went out to the showroom and the dealer introduced Jim as a great Ad Man and special friend to the dealership. "Everyone is excited that Dan Gable is here to speak to us for our regular communications meeting!"

While a relatively small dealership, everyone was there, from the dealer to the sales and F&I team, the business office, operator, the parts team, the service team, the detail crew and even the wash boys.

He continued by saying that his life long experience suggests that the best person to talk about reaching your goals and dominating them would be none other than from the most winning coach in history, our coach, friend and life mentor, Dan Gable.

Jim didn't want to miss a word! He started a new page in his spiral and labeled it at the top "Dan Gable" and started writing as fast as he could.

Dan thanked everyone for starting early today and giving him the opportunity to share. He started by saying, "No speech can take the place of hard work – you learn more from working hard than from anyone's speech." However, he hoped his talk would inspire everyone to work hard and do their best to become the best.

Dan went on to say that over the years it was hard work that persevered to teach him lessons by breaking through obstacles, failures and things that were difficult in life. He reminded everyone that life is full of obstacles, so they needed to be ready to work harder when they encountered those obstacles.

With this the dealer went to the whiteboard and wrote:

L- Listen to others

E- Enthusiastic

A- Apply lessons you learn from listening

R- Recovery time is important

N- Never give up

Develop the Ability to Listen

Dan continued that as an athlete and coach the reason he was able to dominate was the result of a simple formula: "The first skill in a successful life is to develop the ability to listen. People need to listen to the people around them. Usually there are resources around you that are trying to help you if you only learn to listen for and to them. Everyone needs to develop an eagerness to listen and gather feedback from those you encounter."

Be Disciplined to Stay the Course

"Do not stop there. You need to have the discipline to keep staying the course. Especially today, it seems everybody wants instant gratification and success and that never happens. What seem to be overnight success stories usually take years of hard work and discipline to make them happen.   If you keep on working hard every day, listen to those resources around you and keep on applying the lesson learned, eventually you will have success!"

The dealer then wrote on a board the formula:

Listen + Application + Discipline = Success

Active Listening may be Necessary

Dan went on to expand the formula with the following:

Listening is the #1 skill one can have.

With this the dealer took his place at the board and wrote,

> *"Effective questioning brings insight, which fuels curiosity, which cultivates wisdom."- Chip Bell*

Everyone seemed to be taking notes and nodding in agreement. Jim found himself nodding along without realizing it.

Application

Dan continued: "Application is the second skill one must acquire. The ability not only to hear but to apply what you are hearing and learning from listening!" Listening by itself was not enough.

Then the dealer went back to the board and wrote,

"Knowing is not enough, you must apply! Willing is not enough, you must do!"

Recovery Time

Dan talked about recovery. He said recovery was just as important as the hard work because you can burn out. He shared that he worked on allowing his body to recover just as much as he did on working out. This helped him make sure he was ready to do his next workout or compete in the next event. He also found out that the teams that recovered together also won together!

Jim knew Dan was talking about sports teams but this seemed to make sense in business also. This might provide opportunities for team building.

Never Give Up

Dan explained, "I define great leadership different from most. Great leadership to me is about working hard. It is about being the first one there and the last to leave. Then you must believe in what you are listening to. Believing in the formula is also a key to successful application! Believing in your goals keeps you working hard."

The dealer once again appeared and wrote on the board,

"A man lives by believing something:

not by debating and arguing about everything."

Great Leadership is about Hard Work

Dan continued, "Great leaders work hard!"

With that the dealer went back to the board and wrote,

"Leaders aren't born, they are made. And they are made just like anything else, through hard work. And that's the price we'll have to pay to achieve that goal, or any goal." -
Vince Lombardi

Great Leadership is about Having and Casting a Vision

Dan continued, "Leadership is about having a vision and being able to cast that vision. A big part of leadership is trying to think what comes next, along with being creative and trying to be better than everyone else at what you chose to focus on. Visions need to be big. People are likely to follow big visions that are cast with confidence."

The dealer appeared again and wrote on the board,

"People want to be part of something larger than themselves. They want to be part of something they're really proud of, that they'll fight for, sacrifice for, that they trust." — Howard Schultz, Starbucks

Then Dan stated, "The more discipline you have in life, the more elite you will be. The more you master discipline, the better chance for your success in life. Focused discipline makes a big difference."

Great Leaders Persist Until They Dominate

Dan continued, "To dominate, you have to keep on and domination doesn't just happen and very few can dominate. Following the formula daily will give you success and if you keep following this formula, more success will follow."

Preventing Adversity

Gable next talked about adversity. "In all our lives there will be adversity. Having a little adversity can be ok, but if you have a lot of adversity this means you may be on a losing path." He explained that there is no such thing as luck. If you continue to lose, that's on you. That means you are not making the right decisions in life that are necessary to win and maybe not listening enough or applying the right principles. To win you need to be reflecting and learning from your own history. Plan for adversity and then when it happens, you will be ready.

Focus on Lessons Learned from Experiences - Reflection

"You have to focus on what you did right and what you did wrong and apply the lessons learned from those experiences. If you continue to lose and not reflect and make the positive changes required, you enter a downward spiral. You may continue to lose and it becomes harder to pull out of the downward spiral until it eventually becomes a habit and a negative reality," Gable stated.

The dealer then wrote on the board,

" It may be helpful to list TGR-(Things Gone Right) and TGW – (Things Gone Wrong) regularly during your reflection time."

Living in the Present - Recalibration

Next Dan talked about the present, sharing what he learned from his high school teacher and assistant wrestling coach at Waterloo West High School, Bill Blake. He said, "We need to talk about today, the right now. Now is the present - is it good? If not, then you need to understand the past and change the current, until it is good." He said that where we are now is all that we can control. "We can't control the past and the only hope we have to control the future is to control the present. We must continue to recalibrate our life's compass every day to continuously improve. This will also help prevent making the same mistakes. The preparation of the past creates the future successes when it meets opportunity daily," he continued.

Jim had to think about that. Right now, this is my future and if I continue to look back at my past and reflect and then change my present, I can control my future. Today's preparation leads to tomorrow's success.

Jim's thoughts were interrupted by the dealer returning to the board and writing,

"Yesterday is history, tomorrow is a mystery and today is a gift. That is why they call it the present!"

Dan Gable continued on to say that it was easy to be good because most of the standards to be good are set so low. He said it was easy for him because he understood the discipline and how to identify and listen to people who were trying to help. He also found it helpful to apply the lessons of life as quickly as possible.

He went on to talk about the importance of leadership and in any organization like this dealership, you need to have real leadership and you need to adopt a strategy of domination, with a thirst to be the best.

Dan emphasized that morning at the dealership that you need to have leaders and leadership in winning organizations. It is all about being motivated and building passion throughout your team.

Many years later Gable taught these same principles when he visited the Green Bay Packers team to teach leadership lessons, early in the 2010-2011 season in which the Packers went on to win Super Bowl XLV. One of the first

questions he asked Coach Mike McCarthy was who the leaders were on the team. That's where the Green Bay Packers had to start in 2010.

He explained that if they had enough leaders who were willing to pay the price, they could dominate the NFL. The Packers developed those passionate leaders who were willing to listen and adapt their plans based on the lessons they learned that season and won Super Bowl XLV.

Dan continued on to this dealership group saying, "Some of you need to step up and commit to becoming those types of leaders."

Where are the Leaders?

Dan continued, "Are you a leader? Everyone has the opportunity to be or become a leader. Many people don't view themselves as a leader when they should be. No matter what position or how large the group, if the leaders don't have passion, they can't be the best. The leaders who are not motivated cannot become the best or dominate their industry or sport. Their organizations will never achieve their full potential without proper passion or motivation."

Leadership is Always Tested by Adversity

Real leadership is tested when adversity hits and you choose to take it on! When things are hard, difficult, scary and even dark, that is when adversity hits. This is when you have to be the most passionate and become the most motivated. A good leader takes this challenge.

At this point the dealer went to the board and wrote,

Leadership Matters!

Dan continued, "Great leadership should positively affect the masses. Real leadership affects everything and everyone. Leaders come from people working with you, for you, the people you are coaching, the people who surround you, your family, cohorts, friends and associates. A good leader helps others get more out of themselves and the masses that surround them. Leadership to me is getting other people to reach within themselves to get more out of themselves. It is getting them to break barriers, build confidence, getting them to believe they can be the best. It is also getting them to overcome obstacles."

With that the dealer returned to the board and wrote,

"Leadership matters; leadership descends from character."

Dan continued, "Remember, no one is born a leader. It's something that you have to work on, something that is wanted, something that is believed in and something that is focused on daily. You have to believe you can be great and are willing to work hard to accomplish!"

Personal Recovery and Reflection Time

Dan added that each leader, at the end of each day, individually needs to allow time to recover and relax. That was Dan's chance for him to reflect on what he did or what he needed to do better. Dan would ask himself how he can improve on what he did today and how he can become better next time. Dan shared he spent time every day doing what he described as personal reflection. This was where he would think about what was important and what he needed to change or fix.

With this the dealer returned to the board and wrote,

"Personal reflection improves future performance."

Dan reminded them, leadership is about honesty – no one will believe, follow or trust you if you are not honest!

Jim thought that you could look into Dan Gable's eyes and see that he was real, everything about him you could tell was honest, true and genuine!

Jim looked at his notes and highlighted what Dan ended with, "A great leader takes it on!   At no time ever before, have we realized that leadership really does matter!"

With that last point, Dan thanked the employees for allowing him to share some of his ideas with them at this early hour. The entire group rose to their feet and gave him a standing ovation.

Without even being conscious of it, Jim found himself standing and clapping with the employees. The dealer responded by clapping as well. It was in that moment that Jim noticed the "S" ring on the dealer's right hand. This was the same ring that the other dealers, and Dan Gable, were wearing!

As everyone was leaving, Jim asked the dealer how often they had these meetings. The dealer responded that it was usually a couple of times a month. They sometimes had guest speakers like today who helped train the employees and give them life lessons they could apply at work and at home. At other times they did department updates and discussed how everyone was succeeding and making sure everyone was involved in the company, no matter what their position. They would also take that time to recognize any team member for their outstanding and extra effort.

Little did Jim know at that moment that because this group listened, believed and applied what they learned and used discipline for daily review that in a few years, they would become one of the most successful mega dealers in the Midwest!

Jim was excited about what he was learning. Today, at a small dealership, from life lessons that were taught on goals and what it takes to dominate those goals, he could see this type of structure would change his life forever!

As if someone knew the exact time he would walk into his home from the drive, the phone once again began to ring. He quickly hurried over to the phone and answered it. Like the other three days, the voice on the other end explained that he was a friend of John's and he would be honored if Jim could meet him at his store the next morning. Jim quickly and enthusiastically answered affirmatively and hung up the phone.

This dealer was again over 100 miles away in another direction. By now he had grown accustomed to these drives and these meetings. Each one was different and there would be a new and fresh lesson.

Before Jim went to bed he wanted to review and add some additional notes to all the big life lessons he learned at this small dealership that day!

Ad Man Notes – Key Principles / Coach Dan Gable's Lessons today:

- No speech can take the place of hard work.

L- Listen to others
E- Enthusiastic
A- Apply lessons you learn from listening
R- Recovery time is important
N- Never give up

- 1st skill is to develop the ability to listen. Everyone needs to develop an eagerness to listen and gather feedback from those you encounter.

- 2nd skill is to learn to apply the lessons learned while listening. After learning to listen, you have to apply the lessons and keep on applying them on a daily basis!

- Do not stop there. You need to have the discipline to keep staying the course. Then stay disciplined to continue to apply the lessons daily.

- Keep on applying the lesson learned, eventually you will have success!

- Everyone wants_to be good immediately. This never happens.

- Listen + Application + Discipline = Success.

- Active listening may be necessary.

- Great leaders persist until they dominate - To dominate, you have to keep on and domination doesn't just happen and very few can dominate.

- Adversity happens - In all our lives there will be adversity. Having a little adversity can be ok, but if you have a lot of adversity, this means you may be on a losing path.   Reflect and learn from your own history and focus on lessons learned from things gone right and wrong.

- Your past must be constantly re-evaluated and you must change the current until you can say it is good!

- The preparation of the past creates the future successes when it meets opportunity daily.

- Right now, this is my future and if I continue to look back at my past and reflect and then change my present, I can control my future.

- Today's preparation leads to tomorrow's success.

- "Yesterday is history, tomorrow is a mystery and today is a gift. That is why they call it the present!"

- Are you a leader?

- Real leadership is tested when adversity hits and the leader takes it on!

- A good leader helps others positively get more out of themselves and the masses that surround them. It is getting them to break barriers, build confidence, getting them to believe they can be the best. It is also getting them to overcome obstacles.

- "Leadership matters; leadership descends from character."

- No one is born a leader! It doesn't just happen. You have to believe you can be great and are willing to work hard to accomplish.

- Everyone needs to focus their skills and efforts to continually become a better leader.

- A leader, at the end of each day, individually needs to allow time to recover and relax. That was Dan's chance for him to reflect on what he did or what he needed to do better.

- "Personal reflection improves future performance."

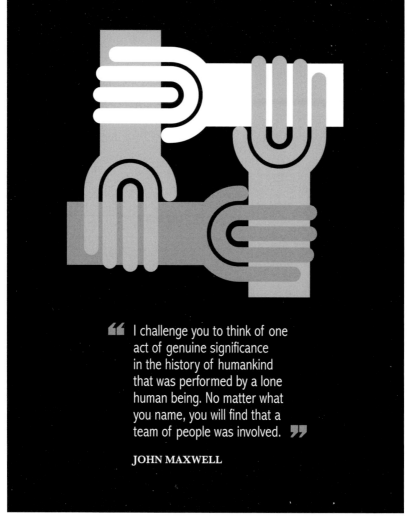

I challenge you to think of one act of genuine significance in the history of humankind that was performed by a lone human being. No matter what you name, you will find that a team of people was involved.

JOHN MAXWELL

Chapter 6

Team Alignment

"You can design and create, and build the most wonderful place in the world. But it takes people to make the dream a reality."

Walt Disney

As he drove in the next morning, he found himself reviewing what had been a wild and exciting week so far. At the beginning of the week, he had felt like he lost a 25-year career. Now, the excitement of the last four days seemed to eclipse any negativity from that. He could hardly sleep last night thinking of all the opportunities that his future might have.

He arrived at the dealership at 6:55 AM. As he pulled up, he did not see the dealer waiting for him this time. He wondered if he was at the right dealership. He reviewed his notes and this was the right dealer and address, but he wondered where the dealer was. He had grown accustomed to having a welcoming party, but not today. He wondered if he had written down the time or date wrong.

He walked in the front door and there was no receptionist. This seemed odd. There was no one on the showroom floor either. Where were the salespeople? He walked all the way through sales and continued to the service department where several voices could be heard. As he entered the service department he saw people everywhere with mops, brooms and trash cans. Water was everywhere.

A gray haired man of medium stature approached him and said, "Jim, good to see you. Sorry about this. Our water pipes busted early last night and most of our employees and some of their family members have been here all night cleaning up. We were able to get sales and the front end cleaned up and we are just about through with the last department clean up."

As Jim looked around, there were dozens at least, maybe 40 or 50 people coming and going. There were even children

Team Alignment

helping with the clean up. The people were joking, laughing and singing as they finished cleaning up the last of the water. The people were dressed in many different ways. About the time Jim finished glancing around, the dealer called everyone together and thanked them for their willingness to work together to get the dealership cleaned up and ready to do business again. He shared that when he had first gotten the news, he had called a couple of his department managers and they called a couple of their reports and they called a couple of their coworkers and before he knew it most of their team was helping. Employees began showing up almost immediately after the calls. Their spouses, children and even some of their customers had shown up to help with the cleanup.

The dealer commented that at his store when the circumstances were at their worst, his people were always at their best. The dealer said, "You know what they say, your test becomes your testimony and your messes become your message." Then he turned to the sales manager who was mopping behind him. "It looks like we are going to have one heck of a water sale today!" With that everyone began laughing.

115

Jim was suddenly aware that he was mopping up too and he couldn't remember when he had even picked up the mop. He thought it odd that he was helping but it seemed right so he kept on mopping.

When the dealership was dry again, they all met in the conference room. On the wall was that big "S" again. Jim had grown accustomed to seeing one at each of the other dealers he had visited.

Since Jim was the only newcomer there, the dealer introduced him as the Ad Man and said he is known as a friend of the auto industry. Everyone clapped to welcome him. The dealer then said he had called Jim earlier yesterday to introduce him to the best team in the world and share his teamwork principles with him. After the pipes burst, the dealer realized Jim may have witnessed the best example of teamwork the dealer could have imagined.

At that point, one of the managers suggested to the dealer that he take Jim on the "teamwork walk" and everybody began to cheer. The dealer smiled and said, "Why don't we all take him on the walk?" With that, another manager opened the door and the crowd began moving to the hall off the showroom.

Then the crowd stopped and pointed at a sign that spelled out the word "team."

T-Together

E-Everyone

A-Achieves

M-More

The dealer spoke, "It all starts with the belief that the sum of everyone is better than any individual and everybody wins more when we work together.   Great teams require trust."

Next, one of the managers pointed to where all the employees had signed on the wall under the words, "We are a TEAM." The manager pointed to the next poster and added, as if on cue, "Good communication is essential to trust and teamwork. This requires listening and discussing many different issues and solutions before making key decisions. Trust has to be the foundation of every successful team."

At the next sign, they stopped and together several of them read, "Many hands make for light work." Someone made a funny remark about last night's team clean up effort. They laughed recalling their all night assault on the water that had taken over the dealership as a result of the burst pipe. The dealer then added, "This is just like a fine clock that only works if all the gears and cogs fit together properly. We have to have the right people in the right place at the right time doing the right things.   When we add our weaknesses to others' strengths and vice versa, we can together achieve more -- and do it quicker too!"

The group moved to the next sign on the wall and it said, "Great leadership is essential to successful team building." The dealer explained that challenging situations usually require several individuals or groups to work together to develop multiple solutions to a problem or obstacle. They need to consider all the available resources while evaluating the potential solutions and the probable results. Developing leaders at every level of an organization can help build effective teams.

The crowd continued moving to the next sign which read "Defined decision- making helps build great teams!" Another manager began to share that when everyone understands the decision-making process and the roles and expectations of the team, the team operates more effectively. He shared that sometimes the team members may not agree and when this occurs one individual team member has to assess all the data and make what he believes is the best choice for the organization. This can be the test of the real trust of the team – do they trust the individual to make the decision in the best interests of the team, and to not do so in a self-serving way. One manager piped in, "Even though there is no "I" in team, a healthy team can function with individuals in it making decisions according to the agreed-upon decision process." Along those lines, the next poster they came to said:

"It's amazing what you can accomplish if you don't care who gets the credit." Harry S. Truman

The final poster they stopped to look at was entitled "The 6 C's of Teamwork":

1. Clear goals and expectations

2. Communication

3. Commitment

4. Competence

5. Collaboration

6. Coordination

The manager closest to the poster explained that clear goals and expectations meant that everyone on the team needed to know what was expected individually and collectively and when things were expected. Team members must realize the importance they play in their individual role in creating the team's success as well as the failure they can cause by not understanding this important principle!

He stressed the importance of communication and continued that commitment must be shared equally by everyone on the team or the team would not be able to enjoy sustained success. Another manager responded that a team needed members with complementary areas of competence required for their roles and that team members work to ensure every part of the organization functioned as it was designed to do and to maximize success.

One more manager spoke up to explain that collaboration was essential to making sure each individual and each team worked with others to deliver the best product or produce the best results. And, he concluded by saying that without coordination, the team would break down and have difficulty completing assignments. This also can lead to frustration among team members and cause the team to fail.

As they continued down the hall, the dealer pointed to the last wall which was covered with signatures. The dealer said after completing their orientation training, they walk each team member down this hall and review the concepts that they feel are important before joining their team. He added, "When we have teamwork issues, we have also found this hall to be helpful with reviewing what being a part of our team was all about. Sometimes a review of what makes effective teams can help boost performance or help resolve issues."

As Jim walked out of the teamwork hall, he noticed another sign on a door that said:

The best strategy to accomplish your goals is

to get team alignment with:

- Identifying what they want to achieve.
- Developing a "blameless" plan.
- Organizing and supporting the team.
- Making sure everyone is taking ownership of the action plan.
- Planning to succeed.

The dealer then added, "Don't play the blame game. It is a weird game where everyone that plays loses! Nobody ever wins at that game."

The Ad Man thought to himself that the poster summed it up very well. He had learned more about teamwork in one day than in his entire previous career. This would definitely be helpful in starting his future teams in his ad agency.

Today had been a vivid demonstration of how a great team worked and what it took to create it. Becoming a great team took goals, structure and hard work and was not likely to be achieved by a group just showing up. He knew that from today's experience, he would never look at a team the same way again.

It was Friday afternoon and this week had been filled with every emotion and a tremendous amount of great advice. He felt like he had had a lifetime of learning in these four short days. He felt blessed to have the opportunity to learn from so many successful business people and he looked forward to their further mentoring. He had gained a whole new respect and admiration for these auto dealers and hoped that he would somehow be able to repay them in the future.

He had also gained a great understanding of the complexity of issues facing auto dealerships with so many departments and employees trying to service their customers with many different wants and needs. Auto dealers were truly among the great American entrepreneurs.

On the drive home today, he also had become increasingly aware of all the makes of vehicles and all the different styles. He thought how many different dealership teams were busy trying to service their customers for their brands and how many employees that must take. This thought seemed mind boggling.

As usual, the phone was ringing as he opened his back door. This time a female voice greeted him as a friend of John's with one more invitation to meet at her dealership on Monday morning. While he was excited to continue his learning, he was exhausted and thankful that he had the weekend to recover and reflect. He had heard of this dealership but had never been there. This dealer had opened a new dealership only three years ago and from what he had heard, their business was growing quickly.

The Ad Man was filled with excitement with his journey just beginning. He knew he needed to spend time with his family and to reflect over the weekend.

Jim began reviewing and summarizing his notes from what he had learned today. He wrote:

Ad Man Notes – Key Principles:

- Your test becomes your testimony and your messes become your message.

- Teamwork walk – we are a TEAM – great teams require trust.

  T – Together

  E – Everyone

  A – Achieves

  M – More

- Real teamwork takes planning.

- Good communication is essential to trust and teamwork.

- Teamwork could be contagious.

- Many hands make for light work.

- Effective teamwork allows individuals and teams to achieve more. [when we add our weakness to others strengths and vice versa, we can achieve more – and do it quicker too!]

- Great leadership is essential to successful team building.

- Defined decision making helps build great teams.

- It's amazing what you can accomplish, if you don't care who gets the credit. Harry S. Truman

- The six C's of teamwork are important to having an effective high performing team.

1. Clear goals and expectations

2. Communication

3. Commitment

4. Competence

5. Collaboration

6. Coordination

- The best strategy to accomplish your goals is to get team alignment with:

    - Identifying what they want to achieve.
    - Developing a "blameless" plan.
    - Organizing and supporting the team.
    - Making sure everyone is taking ownership of the action plan.
    - Planning to succeed.

- Don't play the blame game. it is a weird game where everyone that plays the game loses! Nobody ever wins at that game.

> **"** To succeed, we must
> believe first that we can. **"**
>
> **HENRY WARD BEECHER**

Chapter 7

Reflection

"If you think you'll be a success or think you'll fail – you are probably right"

Henry Ford

Jim had a whirlwind of a week. He spent Saturday catching his wife up on each of the four visits. It helped him remember the important lessons as he recounted them to her. He had taken a lot of notes and he spent time pouring over them and trying to summarize highlights. He took at least one quote from each and had a poster made from them at a local copy store. He planned to place these around his new office so he could start each day with a quote and be reminded of the powerful lessons from each of the visits.

He and his wife also worked on his new office in their basement. She had found some wonderful items – a desk, a conference table and some beautiful bookcases from an estate sale of one of the town's prominent lawyers.   She even hung a plaque right above his desk with a poem from Mother Teresa for inspiration.   The poem read:

People are often unreasonable, irrational, and self-centered.   <u>Forgive them anyway.</u>

If you are kind, people may accuse you of selfish, ulterior motives.   <u>Be kind anyway.</u>

If you are successful, you will win some unfaithful friends and some genuine enemies.   <u>Succeed anyway.</u>

If you are honest and sincere people may deceive you.   <u>Be honest and sincere anyway</u>.

What you spend years creating, others could destroy overnight.   <u>Create anyway.</u>

If you find serenity and happiness, some may be jealous.   <u>Be happy anyway.</u>

The good you do today, will often be forgotten.   <u>Do good anyway.</u>

Give the best you have, and it will never be enough.   <u>Give your best anyway.</u>

In the final analysis, it is between you and God.   <u>It was never between you and them anyway.</u>

This poem was put over Jim's desk, and provided the inspiration that Jim needed just at the right time!

He was now confident his office would look as professional as any agency in town.

Jim could feel himself gaining much needed optimism and as he pondered over all the lessons that he had absorbed, just so far – he began to realize his life was about to dramatically change forever . . . but more importantly he reflected these lessons would also change the lives of many others in years to come and he had a renewed optimism as to what the future might hold.

As Jim talked with his wife, she helped him to think back over his long radio career. He had felt like such a failure on Monday as he sold his share of the business he had loved. As they talked, he was able to think more clearly about his many accomplishments. He had developed one of the best-selling ad campaigns ever for the first radio station he worked for. He had actually been nominated about ten years into his career for a Clio award, the "Academy Awards" for the advertising industry. He did not win it, but just being nominated among the almost 20,000 entries was a success in itself.

His wife helped him think back on the many clients of the radio station who had built their business with his help. He remembered all kinds of business people he had worked with who had complimented him on how he had helped them enhance their business. This gave him a great sense of accomplishment, in spite of how the station had done in the last few months before the sale. He knew that he had contributed to his clients' success and thought that some, if not many of them would be great references for him as he started to woo clients to his new ad agency. He also started making lists of the individuals and companies he had helped who might want his agency's assistance in the coming year. Without even finishing the list, he had over 60 different prospects for his new agency.

So, the combination of focusing on the positive accomplishments from his 25-year radio career (applying the first lesson he learned this week about positive attitude) and the reflection on the many lessons from the four dealers left him feeling inspired and reinvigorated at the end of the weekend. He also reminded himself of one lesson from the past week – it is hard to go forward if you spend too much time thinking of the past.

He remembered growing up on a farm and the one rule of plowing a field was if you wanted straight rows, you had to pick a point in front of you and focus on it. Before he went to sleep he pulled out all his notes from his dealership visits and re-read them over one more time just to refresh in his mind all that he had learned. He was now ready to focus on a point ahead and ready to start another week with an early morning meeting at the next dealership.

> Setting a goal is not the main thing. It is deciding how you will go about achieving it and staying with the plan.

TOM LANDRY

Chapter 8

Accomplishment Requires ACTION

"Success is not forever

and failure isn't fatal."

Don Shula

On the drive over the next morning, Jim, now thinking of himself as the Ad Man reflected on what he thought was one of the most exciting weeks of his life. While it had begun with a big change, most of his energy and thoughts were now focused on the future.

As Jim pulled into the dealership, he noticed that this dealer seemed to have several franchises on adjoining properties.

No wonder their advertising called this dealership the "Auto Mall." As he walked up to the main door for one of the buildings, a very distinguished tall lady walked out and immediately shook his hand. She welcomed him and expressed appreciation for his visit. She apologized for all the construction that was going on all around them but explained that business had been growing by leaps and bounds since they moved to this side of town.

She invited him in to her office and explained that the previous individual that owned this dealership had refused to relocate so she and her father had an opportunity to purchase it. While she had worked for many years helping her father at their other store, this was the first time she was fully in charge. She said that by moving to this side of town, they had increased their sales four-fold over what the previous dealership had sold. On top of that, other franchises were excited about partnering with her at this location.

She then looked at her watch and announced that it was time for the managers' meeting. She explained that once a month, they gathered all the department managers together to discuss a key success principle. She rose out of her chair and led him to the meeting upstairs in their conference room. As Jim looked up, he saw a large staircase and he followed her lead up the stairs. When they opened the door, forty people were already seated in the conference room. She motioned for Jim to take the empty seat which was waiting for him in the front row. She then went to the center of the conference room and thanked everyone for being on time.

She introduced Jim to the group as the Ad Man and a friend of the auto industry. The group welcomed him in unison. She then walked to the whiteboard at the center of the room and wrote:

"Action is required for accomplishment"

She began to remind everyone of the background of the dealership that several years ago when the market had shifted, the previous dealership owner refused to relocate. By the time he was ready to move, it was too late. That provided her and her father the opportunity to open this store. She reported that the last two years their business was growing at 10 times the national average.

She looked around the room and stated, "I have the best team anywhere to seize this opportunity." She continued writing on the board. She then stated, "Action is required for advancement. So many people were waiting to do something while the market and the opportunities were moving on." She then wrote:

"Decisions determine destiny and your focus will determine your future"

She said that in a rapidly changing, competitive environment, the ability to make good decisions quickly makes the difference between profits and losses in every department of the dealership. She also added that making no decision was in fact a decision – and sometimes a perilous one.

She turned back to the board and wrote:

"Fear and procrastination are the two biggest enemies

of effective decision making"

With this, she pointed to a poster in a corner of the conference room, which read:

F- False

E- Evidence

A- Appearing

R – Real

She continued, "Sometimes procrastination is the symptom and fear is the problem. Even if you are on the right track, you will get run over if you just sit there." With that, many people in the room chuckled. She continued, "The problem with trying to always stay in the center of the road on every issue is that you get hit by both sides of the traffic," which again brought a laugh from many in the room.

She explained that fear holds people back from flexing their risk muscles and that fear of the future was a waste of the present. Fear wants us to run from something that isn't there. She then raised her right hand to point to the far wall. As she did so, the Ad Man noticed the light caused a sparkle from an "S" pin on her blouse, the same distinct "S" that was just like other dealers had on their rings. For a second, he again wondered what that "S" stood for but then, he quickly went back to focusing on the quotes on the wall posters.

On the poster she was pointing to was a quote from

Theodore Roosevelt:

"It is not the critic who counts: not the man who points out how the strong man stumbles or where the doer of deeds could have done better. The credit belongs to the man who is actually in the arena, whose face is marred by dust and sweat and blood, who strives valiantly, who errs and comes up short again and again, because there is no effort without error or shortcoming, but who knows the great enthusiasms, the great devotions, who spends himself for a worthy cause; who, at the best, knows, in the end, the triumph of high achievement, and who, at the worst, if he fails, at least he fails while daring greatly, so that his place shall never be with those cold and timid souls who knew neither victory nor defeat."

She stated, "The difference between successful people and people who fail is often their ability and willingness to make difficult decisions and take action quickly. I don't know why people don't jump at opportunities as quickly as they seem to jump to conclusions." That interesting statement caused more appreciating laughter.

She then pointed to another wall poster entitled "Making the Right Decisions" and began to read:

Decisions made easy procedure

1. Identify, understand and discuss the problem

2. Research, list and discuss possible solutions

3. Compare and contrast solutions

4. List pros and cons of solutions

5. Rank order solutions

6. Execute the solution

She said some managers worried too much about any problem and seem to suffer from "paralysis analysis" and would repeatedly put off decisions until the situation blew up. This almost always caused a great deal of collateral damage that could have been avoided if a quick decision were made earlier. She brought more laughter with her comment that "worry was the darkroom where negatives were developed."

She added that good ideas sometimes have a very short shelf life and if not acted on quickly, they tend to expire or rot like unconsumed produce. She said procrastination was not murder; it was business "suicide." She encouraged the group to use the decision-making process and take action quickly and added, "I have hired great managers whom I trust and I have confidence in your decision- making skills."

The dealer said another key principle to remember when dealing with a customer - "Everybody wants cheap – but nobody likes cheap. When drawing the customers' attention, most customers are drawn to what they feel is a good deal or in a sense a low or cheap price, for what they need or want to purchase.   Inevitably, they really don't want cheap and once they are on location ready to buy, they have the tendency to view cheap and prefer to up-grade or up-sell themselves to more than cheap." This concept can be utilized to assist the customer in getting what they really like and what they really want, since you have already done the hard part in using cheap to draw them to your store and then allow and help them up-sell to their needs and wants. They buy and leave very satisfied, happy and appreciative of what the store and people did to help them."

The room seemed to get energized again at her remarks and the excitement level felt almost like a pep rally before the big game. Jim could see why this dealership was outperforming all the competition and setting national records. She concluded with, "Sometimes you have to go out on a limb where the big fruit is. You have to always remain open to new ideas and change. Finally, we can't always do everything at once but we sure can do something at once!"

After the meeting disbanded, Jim spent another hour debriefing with the dealer learning more about their trend-setting approaches for running the dealerships. Having an inside look at a successful dealership like this would definitely help him better understand the needs of other dealers. When he returned home, just like the other evenings, he reviewed his notes and wrote:

<u>Ad Man Notes – Key Principles</u>:

- Action is required for accomplishment.

- Action is required for advancement.

- Decisions determine destiny.

- Fear and procrastination are the enemy of effective decision making.

  F – False

  E – Evidence

  A – Appearing

  R - Real

- Sometimes procrastination is the symptom and fear is the problem – fear wants us to run from something that isn't there.

- The difference between successful people and people who fail is their ability and willingness to make difficult decisions and take action quickly – so, why don't people jump at opportunities as fast as they jump to conclusions?

- Making the right decisions – the decisions made easy procedure:

1. Identify, understand and discuss the problem.

2. Research, list and discuss possible solutions.

3. Compare and contrast solutions.

4. List pros and cons of solutions.

5. Rank order solutions.

6. Execute the solution.

- Worry is the darkroom where negatives are developed.

- Our decisions determine our destiny.

- Critics will always be critical.

- Everybody wants cheap – but nobody likes cheap.

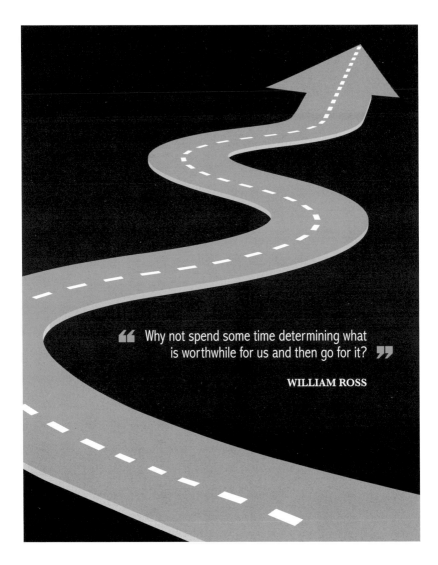

" Why not spend some time determining what is worthwhile for us and then go for it? "

WILLIAM ROSS

Chapter 9

Ask For and Expect

"The results you achieve will be in direct proportion to the effort you apply."

Denis Waitley

As Jim was enjoying his ride to meet the next dealer, he was also enjoying the countryside. He had heard about an annual festival that occurred in the town to which he was driving. Then, he recalled hearing that this dealer was a sponsor of the festival.

When he pulled up to the dealership, the dealer appeared, seemingly from nowhere, to open his car and welcomed him to town. He thanked Jim for coming and invited him to follow him. This man walked hurriedly as if he was on a mission. Jim walked quickly to keep up with him, through the store and all the way back to a conference room they went.

The dealer walked up to the front of the room and pointed to a chair in the front row for Jim to be seated. He thanked everyone for being there so promptly. He then pointed to Jim who was still getting his breath from what seemed like a sprint from his car to the conference room. The dealer said, "This is Jim; he is an advertising man and a friend to the automobile industry and he will be joining us for our meeting today."

With the introduction done, he walked to the board and wrote.

Ask for the order!!

He then began to explain that throughout history, there were examples of great individuals who never succeeded because they didn't take the action needed or ask for the order. They had great potential, great possibility-- if they had just asked for the order.

The dealer then shared that in this business, while demonstrating the product and product knowledge are important, they are not enough to create a successful sales career. The real key to maximizing one's success in sales and in life is asking for the order. He gave examples of his years of working in the dealerships where he had seen many great presenters but they would never get around to inviting the customer to purchase a vehicle. Then he added, "Getting what you want is not always easy. A lot of people spend lots of time planning their future, setting goals and then they don't go after what they want. Sometimes they just wait around hoping that the future they had dreamed about, planned for and set goals about would just appear."

He then went to the board and wrote:

Six key strategies to get the order

- Be assertive.

- Know exactly what you want.

- Know what your client wants.

- Be flexible.

- Be prepared for a "No."

- Understand that basic human nature is to help others.

"Being assertive in a polite way is about combining confidence and control. It can be helpful with obtaining a positive reaction. You have to know what you want and what the client wants. If you are wishy washy, you will likely lose the sale. Your goal is not to make a sale above all. First, you have to understand what the client wants. If you can help provide a solution to their problem, you will be likely to make the sale. But, you must be flexible as you learn more about the client and their needs and desires."

"Be prepared for a possible 'No' as an answer but remember most people want to help you, especially if you are trying to help them. You know what they say; people don't care how much you know until they know how much you care." The dealer concluded, "Remember, if you don't ask, you won't receive." Jim thought to himself how many times he wanted to help others, but if they didn't ask he didn't get that opportunity to provide the help they need.

The dealer went to the board and wrote.

Expect immediate results!

He explained that customers want immediate results whenever possible and their dealership's people were empowered to make decisions and meet the client's needs in many instances.

He went on to say, "All over the world – most of the time in business – people are asking, 'What time is it?' When the real question is, 'What is this time for?'"

He next wrote on the board in big letters.

TAKE ACTION!

He continued, "While it may seem cliché, without action, nothing happens. You know what they say – small deeds done are better than great deeds planned and he who has begun is half the way done. You don't have to be great to get started but you have to get started to be great. It is not what you know but what you do with what you know." He finished with a laugh.

Jim reflected on how important taking action, being assertive and asking for the order would be to starting his new business. His ride home passed quickly as he thought about the lessons the dealer had shared with Jim and his dealership team today.

As with each night last week, the phone was ringing when he opened the door to his home, only this time it was his close client and friend, John. Without John's encouragement to start his own advertising agency and offer to be his first client, he would never have had the incredible experiences of the last week and a half. He might still be moping around, feeling sorry for himself at the ending of his radio career. Instead, he was confident that the many successes he had during the first career in radio would provide a firm foundation for his success running an ad agency.

John asked how his visits had been. It was just over a week from their meeting last Monday when John offered to become his first client. As he began to share some of what he had learned over the week, the lessons just seemed endless. He told John he felt a bit like he had been drinking water out of a fire hose but he was incredibly thankful. He shared with John that he had taken at least a hundred pages of notes that he was sure would be invaluable to him in the future.

John patiently waited as Jim talked and listened as he shared the many things he had experienced and the excitement this journey had provided him at just the right time. At this point, the total experience of the last week seemed to overcome him and he paused to regain his composure.

John asked him if they could meet later in the week, Thursday, for breakfast. John told Jim that he wanted to hear more about the visits and discuss some other ideas with him as well. They agreed to meet in the back dining room of the Angus Restaurant at 7:00 AM for breakfast.

As Jim hung the phone up, he found himself again wanting to share with his wife everything he had learned and experienced this week but she and the kids had already gone to bed. It would have to wait until tomorrow.

Before he went to bed, he took time to reflect on key notes from today's lessons and experiences while they were still fresh in his mind. He also took notes on some of the interrelationships between the different concepts he was learning – something that had occurred to him during his reflection time over the past weekend.

As Jim began to review and then summarize this day's lessons he wrote:

Ad Man Notes – Key Principles:

- Ask for the order.

- You can't get an order if you don't ask. – 6 key strategies to get the order.

    1. Be assertive.

    2. Know exactly what you want.

    3. Know what your client wants.

    4. Be flexible.

    5. Be prepared for a "No."

    6. Understand that basic human nature is to help others.

- "All over the world – most of the time in business – people are asking, 'What time is it?' When the real question is, 'What is this time for?'"

- Take action and expect ∧ immediate results.

  Great

- You don't have to be great to get started but you have to get started to be great!

- If you are moving and looking forward, you don't have time to dwell on the past.

- Be assertive.

- People want to help people.

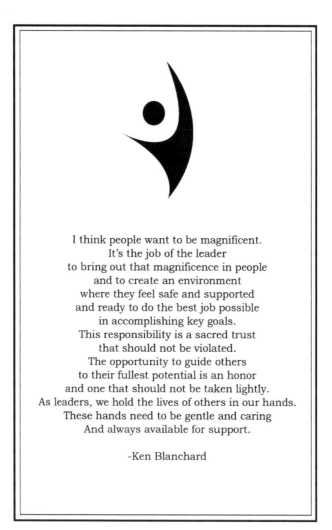

I think people want to be magnificent.
It's the job of the leader
to bring out that magnificence in people
and to create an environment
where they feel safe and supported
and ready to do the best job possible
in accomplishing key goals.
This responsibility is a sacred trust
that should not be violated.
The opportunity to guide others
to their fullest potential is an honor
and one that should not be taken lightly.
As leaders, we hold the lives of others in our hands.
These hands need to be gentle and caring
And always available for support.

-Ken Blanchard

Chapter 10

PRAISE

"You get what you reward."

Author Unknown

As Jim entered the small town, he saw only one stop light. Down Main Street, just like the caller had said, was the biggest business in that small town: Main Street Motors.

As Jim drove in, he saw the signs for employee parking. But he noticed something different about them. The signs said, "Parking for Main Street Motors Stars – our employees." The parking was easily accessible for all employees and was right at the front of the building. This was unusual. At many stores he had visited, the employee

After that, the dealer had the managers from each department stand up and talk about what each of their department's employees had achieved. Jim watched as each employee's accomplishments were described in detail and he noticed how energized everyone got! Finally, the employees took their turn recognizing both managers and peers for what they had done to help them. At the end of this session, the employees left the conference room like a high school football team preparing to take the field at the state football championship. It was almost electrifying to see.

After a tour of the facility, the dealer asked Jim if he would like to go somewhere they could talk some more. Jim eagerly accepted as he was excited to learn more about this dealer and his team. The dealer pulled his car up and motioned for Jim to hop in and the next stop was the Sunset Grill. As they walked in, a waitress came running up and gave the dealer a hug and introduced herself to Jim as one of the dealership's former employees. She seemed so glad to see him. This seemed strange to Jim that a former employee would be so enthusiastic to see her previous boss. He thought to himself there has to be a story here.

As Jim and the dealer were seated, the dealer told Jim that the waitress had been one of their best salespeople ever. But, she had a dream to open her own restaurant and after leading Main Street Motors in sales for seven years, she had saved enough to open this diner. The dealer said, "While I hated to lose her for our dealership, I was happy to see her achieve her dream." The dealer continued, "I want to share with you the Main Street Motors philosophy. We believe our people are our greatest asset and everything we do has to be based on that core value. We have found happy employees equal happy customers and that makes the accounting side of our dealership happy!" With that the dealer got a big smile on his face. Jim knew exactly what he meant. Jim could see this – the enthusiasm in the dealership was literally contagious.

The dealer continued, "Sometimes businesses say the customers come first and that sounds great but if the employees aren't happy, then that strategy fails. We have found that without the employees in the equation, the customers will suffer in the long run. You might say our balance sheet depends on our employees executing their jobs enthusiastically and efficiently. I understand that good processes can render consistency, but in our business, it takes people to deliver results consistently! We train our people on our philosophy and time tested processes all the time but our secret weapon is our great team made up of Great Enthusiastic People! And, we've incorporated this truism with great results into our culture: When you take care of the people – [*our employees*] – they'll take care of the customers – and the customers will take care of the business!"

You know what Teddy Roosevelt said, "People don't care how much you know, until they know how much you care!"

"We also found that no amount of money can replace taking time to recognize our people in front of their peers! Early on we struggled with keeping our people motivated. It seemed when things were great and business was good that most of them were happy, but some still were not. When business was bad, everyone was struggling to stay positive. Then, we stumbled on the idea of our PRAISE often program." PRAISE is an acronym for:

P -   People

R-   Recognition

A-   Always

I-   In

S-   Sight of

E-   Everyone

"Our management team started doing this, and like magic, the employees' attitudes got better. After awhile, their attitudes weren't tied to an up or down market, day, month or year but to the amount and frequency of positive praise they received. Our rule is simple: praise in public, correct in private. The ratio we prescribe to our managers is 10 praises for every correction. We also ask them to correct only one thing a day. This allowed the manager to coach without overloading the employees with too much negative stuff. At first, some of our managers questioned the rule about only one correction a day. But, I reminded them with 200 working days or so that represented a chance to fix 200 things a year for each employee. And, with our 10 to 1 rule, well, that meant that the same employee could get 2000 praises in that same year. I have to admit that at first some of the managers found it hard to identify 10 praises for every correction but today our managers have mastered that skill. A great side benefit is that our average tenure is 12 years and our turnover is less than five percent a year. This has reduced our employee training and retraining costs too. PRAISE can be powerful if used correctly."

"According to a study I once read, the number one reason for employees leaving a job, position or company was that the employee didn't feel appreciated or valued. Most people think it is because of money, it is not! We decided to make recognition part of our business strategy and corporate culture. Some of our managers would ask why we were recognizing them for doing their job when they felt like we were paying them enough. They thought their compensation should be their reward and recognition. But, we convinced them that praise and recognition cost little but accomplished a lot. I found that just as you have to train employees to do their job, we had to train our management team on how to properly recognize employees and how to tie in rewards to get the most bang for our buck. We also had to train them on making PRAISE timely and specific. We trained them to tell the employee what they did right and how much it was appreciated and how that behavior could lead to positive outcomes. We also encouraged them to PRAISE the things they wanted duplicated in other employees. We especially wanted to recognize publicly employees who were living out the mission statement in their day to day activities!"

People aren't born understanding how to PRAISE others correctly. The quickest way to make this concept a real part of your life is to first make or create a checklist of people you admire, people who matter to you, in personal and professional circles. Then start checking off that list of their praises you give them until it becomes a habit that you formed.

The dealer also added that companies that were rated most effective in recognizing excellence in their employees saw their return on equity as well as return on assets tripled in comparison to those organizations that were rated lowest in recognition. As Jim could see, it just made good business sense.

Even as the dealer was talking and Jim was trying to take notes, he found himself thinking of times when he ran the radio station where the PRAISE method could have been helpful in motivating the employees. He thought this could also be used for parenting and could not wait to get home to share this new approach with his wife. While he realized it might take some time to master this new approach, he also believed it could pay out in long term dividends by having happier employees. You could certainly feel the difference in attitude in this dealer's employees.

Just then Jim's thoughts were interrupted by the dealer asking another question: "Do you know what the problem is with most businesses?" Jim thought for a little while as the dealer continued, "We implement a pay plan that doesn't line up with the results we want and then we wonder why we can't get everyone to do something else that they aren't getting paid for. We struggled with that one for a while. We decided to implement a pay for performance plan but we reward doing the right things and getting the right results, not just getting the right results. While pay and rewards can be earned for getting the right results, advancement can only be earned by getting the right results and doing the right things. We found that getting the right results at any cost just cost too much. This too took some time for everyone to trust and believe in." The dealer leaned over and winked at Jim and said, "Now our accounting department and the bank love this strategy." Jim was growing more excited about the idea of earning more by doing the right things.

The dealer also said softly, "You can get the right results by doing the right things at the right time with the right motivation but more importantly, you will earn the right to expect everyone else to do the right things also. And, the right thing is the right thing even if everyone is against it and the wrong thing is the wrong thing even if everyone is for it. There is never a wrong time to do the right thing." Jim thought to himself how right this dealer was.

 While hardly taking a breath, the dealer continued that earlier in his career, he had put all his focus on doing things right, not necessarily doing the right things. His time, focus and efforts were on execution of the task and not selecting the right tasks. He then added that even a flawlessly executed plan with problems won't get the results that a poorly executed but correct plan will. He said that many businesses today confused doing things right with doing the right things and they just weren't the same.

Again Jim thought this dealer was right! He could see where time and efforts should be balanced with doing the right things the right way! He thought how many times in his life he got off track on doing things right, not necessarily doing the right things and certainly it did not render the right results. He could see clearly now they weren't the same.

As Jim drove back home that night, he ruminated over the volume of information and ideas he had gathered that day. He would have to take some time and review his notes. As he was walking in the door, the phone rang. His wife smiled and winked and said it was for him.

Ad Man Notes – Key Principles:

- People are your greatest asset – everything is based on that core value.

- The secret weapon is a great team made up of great enthusiastic people.

- Take care of the people who are your employees – they'll take care of the customers – and the customers will take care of the business!

- People don't care how much you know, until they know how much you care! Teddy Roosevelt

- No amount of money can take the place of recognizing the people in front of their peers!

- The Praise Program.

  P – People

  R – Recognition

  A – Always

  I – In

  S – Sight of

  E – Everyone

- Rule – praise in public – correct in private – 10 to 1 Ratio.

- Create a checklist of people you admire, people who matter to you, in personal and professional circles. Then start checking off that list of their praises you give them until it becomes a habit that you formed.

- Pay for performance – but reward for the right things and the right results.

- There is never a wrong time to do the right thing!

- Beware of the trap of focusing on doing things right and not necessarily doing the right things!

Be ready when opportunity comes.
Luck is the time when preparation
and opportunity meet.

ROY D. CHAPLIN, JR.

Chapter 11

The Meeting

"We are all faced with a series of great opportunities brilliantly disguised as impossible situations."

Charles R. Swindoll

Thursday morning Jim got up at 5 AM because he was so excited he could hardly sleep and he did not want to be late for his meeting with John. All he could think and talk about were the two weeks' experiences.

His wife and kids had been happy to see Jim re-energized again. The kids weren't sure exactly what had happened to their dad this past week, but he had been in a great mood.

His wife knew that the experiences had been transformational and his family was enjoying the benefits. Life was great around their home and the future looked bright. Jim seemed to have more pep in his step and was singing around the kitchen as he was helping prepare the kids' breakfast. His wife joked that she was sure glad he was becoming an Ad Man and not a singer or they just might starve to death. The Ad Man and the kids all laughed together.

About that time, Jim looked at his watch and realized it was time to leave. He exclaimed, "I can't keep my only client waiting!" He kissed his wife and kids and headed for his car. As he tried to start his car, the battery was dead and he returned to the kitchen where his wife was waiting with the keys to the minivan. She reminded him he had been meaning to get that battery fixed and he laughed, saying, "I think I know just the dealer to help us." They both smiled.

Jim pulled up to the restaurant just as his friend was arriving. The dealer waved and Jim waited for him to catch up. The dealer told him they could get to the private room quicker if they went around back. They entered a door that said "employees only." The dealer nodded to Jim that it was okay to enter. With that he reached in his pocket, pulled out a set of keys to open the door and they both went in.

When they entered the room, Jim was surprised to see that all the dealers he had met with during the past 10 days were already sitting down eating. The female dealer said, "Last one in buys." The room erupted with their laughter. John said, "It's okay. I know the owners." The big truck dealer said, "You know this is a working breakfast so you guys better catch up." The two took their places at the round table and began eating as if trying to catch up with the rest of the group.

As they all were catching up with each other, Jim thought it seemed like an old hometown family reunion. They were laughing and joking and sharing about their families and their dealerships. By the tone of their conversations, the auto dealership business must be experiencing a boom time.

After about 20 minutes, John stood up and tapped his spoon on a glass of water. With that, one of the dealers went to the far door and pulled on it as if to ensure it was shut and locked. Several of the other dealers began to clear the tables. Jim realized something strange; there were no waiters or bus boys or anyone other than the dealers and him in this room. For a second, he wondered how the food got there and he now recalled each of the people taking turns refilling the coffee. Something is really different here, he thought to himself.

John formally welcomed everyone and said, "Well, I am glad to get everyone back together today. I want to thank you for helping my friend Jim, the Ad Man, with learning the keys to success." He looked directly at Jim and acted very serious for a moment and said, "There will be tests and exams but we don't administer them, the market will. They grade your answers quickly also." Everyone in the room gave a brief smile or chuckle at that remark.

John continued, "We have shared with you our respective views on the recipe for success and we are all impressed with your attitude and interest in learning and applying these principles. But, that is not the only reason why we are here today." With that, everyone stood up and toasted with their water glasses and right there, he saw it again, they each had a ring on their right hand with a big "S" on it! Jim could hardly take his eyes off their rings. As they were returning to their seats, he kept wondering what the big "S" stood for.

The dealer continued highlighting the key areas the Ad Man had learned about over the past week or so including positive thinking, perseverance, goal setting, teamwork and taking action, among others. He added that, "Companies as well as individuals should do business with those who are in the business of doing business." He then commented that while these are the keys to long term and sustained success of any business or organization, there was still more to be learned. Jim had been so focused on those lessons; he felt that the success formula seemed very complete. But, he continued to be amazed at what these dealers had taught him and was excited to learn more. While he knew it would take time to master the principles he had learned, he wondered what else John was referring to.

While Jim was deep in thought about the other areas John was alluding to, John turned to him and asked, "Do you have any questions?" Jim was not usually at a loss for words but this caught him off guard for a moment. After a brief pause, he took time to thank each of them for sharing three of their most precious commodities with him, their time, talent and touch during the last week came at just the right time in his career transition. Then, for a moment, as if the filter on his brain failed, he blurted out, "I do have a question for all of you. What is the significance of the big "S" on your rings and throughout your stores?" All of a sudden, he was embarrassed and he sat back down.

John patted him on the back and said, "Don't be embarrassed, my friend. We hoped you might get around to asking about that. We try not to talk about that too much until we are sure the individual is ready to hear the message. The "S" is not for a fraternity or a school that we all attended as some have guessed in the past. It is not a secret society as others have speculated. It doesn't stand for successful as even more have surmised. It is much more than that." At that, several of the dealers chuckled – having personally heard each of these speculations. "Does the "S" stand for success?" asked Jim. "Not exactly," John continued, "It represents a shared belief and life philosophy that we all have and have used to achieve our success."

With this, he reached under the table and pulled out of a circular tube a large scroll. As he began to unroll it, Jim saw many signatures on the bottom and large words on the top. He could not read the words from where he was sitting. John pointed to the large words on the top of the document. He could see it now as John turned it around.

SERVING OTHERS LEADS TO SUCCESS!

SHARING WITH OTHERS LEADS TO SIGNIFICANCE!

Under each of these statements there were many signatures. He could recognize some of the signatures to be the dealers he had visited over the last two weeks.

"The giant "S" that you saw is a reminder that we are called to serve others and to share with others. We wear a ring to remind us of our commitment to follow these two strategies in our businesses and personal lives!"

Jim marveled at the simplicity of those two strategies. He thought to himself what a wonderful world it would be if more people would adapt the "S" strategy for business and life. John then looked directly at Jim and said, "We want you to join us in our quest. We want to help you build your advertising company and we want you to help us serve others. We have discussed you and your opportunity. If you decide to join our team, you will be asked from time to time to share the principles of success with others."

Jim nodded his head in agreement and began circling the room shaking hands and hugging everyone in the room. While Jim had received many honors in his 25 years of radio, none of them seemed even close to this honor. His eyes began to fill with tears as he reflected on the last couple of weeks and all that had taken place. It seemed almost like a dream. A dream that had come true!

John then asked him to share with the group about his vision and plans to start a new and different kind of advertising company. At least this question he was prepared for, as he had expected that John wanted to hear about it when they met for breakfast. John had put so much trust in him to become his first client and set up all these incredible meetings. Jim just did not know he would have such a large audience for his message. But, then, ad men are all about messages, he mused.

Jim began to share his vision of creating an advertising company with a different approach. His vision had several elements. First, he wanted to focus on the individual customer's mindset, not primarily the dealer's perspective. His approach would include a strategy to answer customer questions and solve a prospective customer's problems. The solutions to a customer's problems could be solved by the products at the dealerships he worked with. Underlying his vision, he explained his philosophy, learned from the lessons of the past two weeks that problems were just opportunities to excel and that solving a customer's or a client's problems would lead to more customers/clients. He was sure that word-of-mouth advertising would help to spread the good news about his new agency.

His specific media strategy included several prongs. One was vertical saturation, placing ads on multiple stations at the same time. Another prong was helping clients determine the right formula for the message at the right frequency using different media, based on a client's desired objectives and budget. Jim believed his clients could quickly have success at getting their message across and that it would lead to increased sales and market share. A third prong was his decision to focus primarily on the automotive dealerships. This was a decision he would have felt was too risky a week ago that now seemed perfect.

Jim summarized, "I don't mean to make it sound simplistic but I think that if I can help dealers determine the right message at the right time the right number of times to the right audience, they will reap the benefits as the market responds with more sales than their competition."

With that, John said, "That sounds like a plan. We will be here for you to provide advice and support as you start this new journey." With that, the meeting began to conclude as the dealers left the breakfast for their businesses to start their work day.

As he was leaving, one of the dealers in the room mentioned that he had a friend at NADA – the National Automotive Dealer Association – that he would like to have Jim meet. He believed that this new and radically different approach to marketing and advertising would draw interest from dealers everywhere. He shared that if Jim could share his ideas in a national speech to dealers at NADA, it would really launch his agency fast. He would probably obtain some additional clients and might just help change the way automotive advertising would be done in the future. He agreed to call his friend at NADA tomorrow about the potential for Jim speaking at the next NADA yearly conference.

As Jim drove home, he reminded himself how blessed he was to have so many terrific people helping him to get his new advertising company started. When he arrived home, it was almost lunch time. He sat with his wife and began to share about the morning's meeting and how it built on the incredible experiences of last week that they had discussed over the past weekend. In particular, he shared his vision for his new advertising company. He also talked about his ideas for using different approaches than the other agencies used and his goals for building the business. He was especially interested in telling her about all the caring leaders he had met and their quest to help others. He could not wait for her to get to meet them. Last, but not least, he showed her his new "S" ring and explained its significance.

She told him how happy she was to see her husband energized again about his work and his goals. He had definitely embarked on an exciting mission. She knew one thing for sure, with all this enthusiasm and passion, Jim had truly become The Ad Man!

<u>Ad Man Notes –</u>

"Companies as well as individuals should do business with those who are in the business of doing business."

<u>The Ultimate Key Principle</u>:

"Serving others leads to success!

Sharing with others leads to significance!"

APPROVED

Permanence, perseverance, and persistence in spite of all obstacles, discouragements, and impossibilities: It is this that in all things, distinguishes the strong soul from the weak.

THOMAS CARLYLE

Chapter 12

JMA Advertising, Inc.

"Nothing in this world can take the place of persistence. Talent will not; nothing is more common than unsuccessful people with talent. Genius will not; unrewarded genius is almost a proverb. Education will not; the world is full of educated derelicts. Persistence and determination alone are omnipotent. The slogan "press on" has solved and always will solve the problems of the human race."

Calvin Coolidge

The next morning, Jim began his first day running his new company by writing down his goals.

- Create an advertising company to serve automobile dealers and other clients that focus on and deliver results using a scientific approach and data from consumers.

- Create leading edge campaigns that maximize technology to deliver systematic and immediate results for his customers utilizing our unique formula for success.

- Work every day to add clients.

- Treat employees in a way as to become an employer of choice.

- Serve others in a way that the clients and customers would be surprised and delighted.

- Long term goals for the agency were:

  - Attain $1,000,000 a year in billings.

  - Create $1,000,000 in Agency Gross Income.

  - Earn $1,000,000 a year in net profit.

He shared these with his wife and they discussed the goals and his plan. She gave him feedback on his plan and he revised some of his ideas. They both had a new-found excitement for his work and she was confident he would succeed. He made a poster with his goals and posted them on the wall of his basement. Jim took the opportunity to share his goals with many of his friends and some of his clients. Most would nod their heads and smile to be polite but he could tell they thought that his goals were dreams. He focused on developing a plan for achieving those goals and he posted them where everyone could see them! He wanted everyone to know he was planning to achieve his goals and his dreams. He was committed to working as hard as he could to make the posted goals a reality!

Over the next few days, Jim began calling some of his previous radio clients and sharing his goals and plan for the new advertising company [*Every goal except the monetary goals, as Jim thought it would be best to keep these goals to himself*]. He also began calling every automobile dealership within 100 miles and setting up appointments to meet with the dealer principals and the general managers.

It was not easy at first. Many explained that they already had someone handling their advertising. Jim would thank them for their time and ask if he could follow up with them in a few months. Jim tracked his numbers and the first week he made 45 calls and had 20 appointments. He had actually obtained one new client.

While he was still excited, cold calling and setting up so many appointments took a lot of energy. Jim knew persistence would be an important part of his strategy for his new company. It was evident from the many lessons he had learned in the two weeks of dealer meetings. Jim was confident the lessons would be the building blocks for this new company.

Jim continued to pursue new clients over the coming months. One day he was excited to receive a call from the dealer who had mentioned a contact at NADA. He had almost forgotten about the dealer's promise to call NADA and try to get Jim on the agenda for their meeting. The dealer said, "Jim, I need you to write your philosophy down and the key points you would present to the dealers at the NADA show so I can pitch you to the NADA meeting program committee." Of course, Jim agreed and promised to send it to the dealer by the following Monday. However, Jim wondered how he would pay for the trip because money was tight with his kids and his wife to provide for.

He was still in the early stages of launching his new company where he was investing in calls, meetings, equipment for his office and more. There seemed to be too much month at the end of the money lately. Even though he had been able to attract new projects and service a few new clients, he would not get paid for 45 to 60 days after helping with each of these ad campaigns.

A few weeks after the initial contact about NADA, the dealer got back in contact with Jim and NADA had approved his speech. They would pay for a hotel room and travel expenses. The meeting was coming up a few months later. Jim thought this could be the break he needed to acquire enough clients to really get his business off the ground.

For the NADA meeting that February, Jim's oldest son and a friend who was joining Jim's company drove a motor home from Iowa down to New Orleans and parked it in the hotel parking lot. This became Jim's mobile office. His staff took turns showering in the one hotel room provided by NADA everyday. While the scheduling took some planning, everything worked out fine. Jim and his wife would get ready early in the morning and the rest of them would use the room after that to get ready. They actually brought prospective clients to the motor home and had meetings all day and into the night. Jim was able to make many good contacts at the meeting. His friend and son were busy also working the convention exhibit floor talking to everyone that would listen and capturing business cards for follow up.

When Jim returned to Iowa, he had a lot of qualified leads but they were all over the country and he didn't even have a credit card to which he could charge his travel expenses if he wanted to visit them. He sat down with his wife and reflected with her again his vision for making a different customer-focused advertising company. He then shared that the NADA trip had given him prospects but he didn't have the cash to travel around and see them. They talked about what would happen if he didn't make some sales quickly. Their already very limited savings would be gone.

She held his hand and said, "We are in this together and we will make this work. Maybe you could offer one day consultation visits where the prospect would pay for travel expenses but you wouldn't charge a fee to them. During this visit, you could provide a free analysis of their current advertising plan and offer some alternatives. That should land you some new clients."

He could sense her concern about taking care of the kids with no money coming in and knew she was struggling to hold back tears. He felt blessed to have such a supportive partner and thought that the plan she suggested just might work. The next days were filled with hours on the phone selling this one day free analysis if the prospect would only pay his travel expenses. He called everyone that they had met at the NADA show and several agreed to his proposition. The appointments were scheduled over the next six months to limit his out of pocket expenses. Jim did not charge them for his meals, although many of the prospects bought his lunch. To limit the number of hotel nights away, he would leave early and get home late to make his plan work. He also had another problem, because he didn't have a credit card, he couldn't rent a car so he had to plan on having the dealer prospects pick him up at the airport closest to them. However, instead of seeing this as a hardship, Jim saw the opportunity to ride with a dealership employee as the opportunity to learn about the dealer's business. So even though Jim needed the rides, due to his financial situation, they ended up being helpful in understanding the dealership as he worked to prepare a thorough analysis of each dealership's current strategy.

Unfortunately, while visiting the dealers was a great long term strategy for his business, it still took awhile to build relationships and to position himself to replace their current agency or advertising arrangement when they were ready to do so. So, it did not result in a lot of short term clients. Jim could definitely see it would help him obtain his long term goals and he was trying to be patient, but he needed current cash flow to pay his bills. As a result, he decided to vary from his goals and his desired market niche somewhat to attract clients who were not automotive companies. Then, he was able to obtain a local restaurant as a client and he managed their TV advertising campaign. This gave him a chance to learn about another industry and provided some cash to get by while he was developing his automotive clients as well.

Jim also created some brochures for various local professional groups and businesses. Jim even landed a pest control company and a bowling alley as clients. Jim was trying his best to apply the lessons he learned in the few weeks before he launched his business, but his business still struggled. Many companies – in all fields – were not used to paying much for advertising or they were tied to organizations they had worked with for many years. They did not really understand or in some cases, want to listen to what was different about Jim's approach and his company. As a result, Jim's company struggled to survive and he struggled to provide for his family. In fact, in the first ten years, the company's net income for the whole ten year period was less than $50,000 total after he paid himself and staff, materials and other costs for his business.

However, somehow the bills got paid and at the end of the first 10 years, the business had grown to five employees and they were doing brochures, direct mail, radio, television and newspaper campaigns for about 50 different clients. While Jim stayed focused on his vision and the goals he had developed 10 years before, most of what he had hoped for had not yet been achieved.

He continued to work hard and there were months when he struggled to pay his bills. However, his and his employees' hard work got them through the tough times. These tough times forced him, as in the early days of the business, to use his creativity instead of capital. Although the business struggled a lot, those lessons he learned from the dealers kept him going and the client list kept growing. Just as importantly, every one of his employees and his family believed in the business and its potential.

Jim was amazed at the team he was building and the way they all worked together to make the impossible possible. He was so proud of them, their effort and the quality of work they produced. They had developed a team that was customer focused that really did get excited about helping their clients produce results. They developed the slogan: "We love it when you succeed!" That became the theme for the agency – which their clients loved too. They developed a strategy based on research that was very effective at getting the attention of their clients' prospects at the right time. They also developed a reputation for having very creative messages that lead to a "Now" market - people ready to purchase a vehicle today.

The agency continued to grow and at the end of 20 years of business, the number of employees had grown to 25. By now, several of Jim's sons had joined the team as well. It was an exciting time. The agency had become profitable and the business was growing exponentially. The agency had become a business that was continually improving and learning from today to produce more tomorrow. Jim was proud that they were dedicated to listening, studying, analyzing and reporting the science behind the art of truly engaging customers. They had become adept at drawing a light to an exact market of those with a predisposed interest in buying at that very moment.

Jim was also proud that their agency had developed a solid, data-based approach to what most of the competitors called an art. This differentiated them from most of the competitors bidding against them and their business continued to grow. Their scientific approach to the deployment of the creative messages allowed them to obtain results faster for their clients while eliminating the wasteful part of non-effective advertising.

Jim took great pride in sharing with his prospects his agency's unique strategy. While other agencies were using a shotgun approach, he was hunting with a rifle and he would explain that. He would also remind these clients that they needed to be shooting at the right target also. The "spray and pray" strategy was becoming obsolete and was far too expensive for companies to use. The agencies that refused to change were going out of business at an accelerated rate.

Jim's agency was on the leading edge of using intelligent strategies to look at the "mass" beneath the water to determine the buying behaviors of potential customers for their clients at the right time. They developed a proprietary approach to obtain advice from their clients' customers and used a solid research-based process to extract this data at the right times. This was a new and different approach in an advertising industry that had been ruled for years by companies that bragged that advertising was more art than science.

More recently, over the past ten years as the company aged from 20 to 30 years in business, the company grew to 165 employees and the agency expanded its business significantly. Jim's children became the leaders of the company and Jim was amazed at how blessed he was to have the entire family playing an active role and using their individual talents to help grow their business. All of his children had learned the secrets that his mentors had shared with him. They were doing business as it should be done.

The agency did accomplish all of the Ad Man's original goals, plus some. Jim got to see his vision realized! He was proud of all the awards they won over the years and that they had become an employer of choice in their community. Most of all, he was proud of how his family had grown together and worked as a team to grow the business.

As Jim reflected back to the days when it all started and especially to how tough the first ten years were, he thought to himself, "Your tests really do become your testimony and your messes do become your message." He also reminded himself of the importance of the "S" mission and sharing with others.

66 History has demonstrated that the most notable winners usually encountered heartbreaking obstacles before they triumphed. They won because they refused to become discouraged by their defeats. 99

B.C. FORBES

Epilogue

"The best thing about the future is that it comes only one day at a time."

Abraham Lincoln

The Ad Man started an advertising agency primarily focused on automobile dealers the very same year he had "failed" in the radio business. Over the years, his number of employees grew from one to several hundred. Armed with the principles he had learned and a spirit of continuous improvement, he was able to serve literally thousands of clients, not only in the United States but globally.

The news of this strategically different advertising and marketing approach spread throughout NADA and among the dealers everywhere. They became known as a results-oriented organization that always seemed to be on the leading edge with a simple formula but also one that was not afraid to embrace new technologies to help their clients grow their business. Their motto became: "We love it when you succeed!"

The Ad Man believed that if they used the advertising formula of an exciting, honest and true "value message," followed by a great vehicle at a great price and ended with a call to action, prospective customers would respond positively. He also was equally certain that consistent frequency of ads would cause a multiplication effect leading to more customers purchasing vehicles quicker. Third, he believed that the message should be delivered on several different mediums at the same time. Limiting the mediums could limit the results. Finally, he also believed that all used car advertising should focus on products by starting with lowest priced vehicles and ending with most expensive – in a single column from the top of the page to the bottom of the page in the paper. This would help capture and retain more prospects' attention for longer periods of time. This "formula" has been successful throughout the agency's history.

The Ad Man continues to learn from his clients today as he is serving them. He has expanded the company to serve other type of clients, in addition to automobile dealers. The agency now serves academic institutions such as universities and colleges, tourism departments, state governments, the entertainment industry and even professional sports teams.

Through the success of the advertising company, the Ad Man and his family have been able to share with others their blessings. The Ad Man shared all that he had learned with his children and today they have continued the legacy of serving others to be successful and sharing with others to do significant things! His family continues to be supportive of his dreams and vision today.

By writing this book, the Ad Man is fulfilling the promise made in the beginning to share with others the principles of success and the "S" secret.

SERVING OTHERS LEADS TO

SUCCESS!

SHARING WITH OTHERS LEADS TO

SIGNIFICANCE!

With that, the Ad Man looked at his calendar and the thought for the day was:

"There is a destiny that makes us all brothers. No man goes on his way alone. All that we give into the lives of others comes back into our own."   *Edwin Markham*

This brought back many memories and made the Ad Man smile.

The Ad Man has been blessed by many wonderful clients over the years and wanted to thank them by sharing this story with them! They were truly the best part of his story. They made the entire story possible. If you are reading this book, you are part of the Ad Man's story as well.

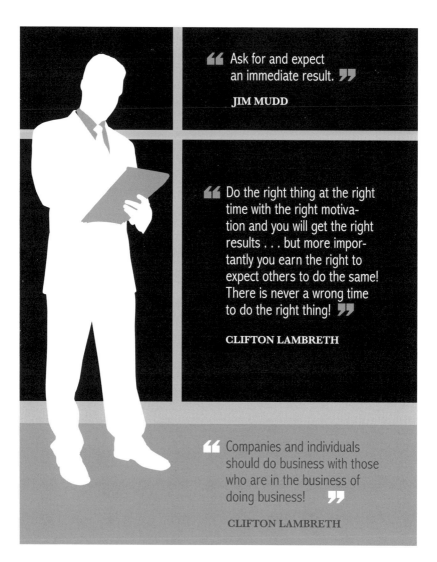

❝ Ask for and expect
an immediate result. **❞**

JIM MUDD

❝ Do the right thing at the right
time with the right motivation and you will get the right
results . . . but more importantly you earn the right to
expect others to do the same!
There is never a wrong time
to do the right thing! **❞**

CLIFTON LAMBRETH

❝ Companies and individuals
should do business with those
who are in the business of
doing business! **❞**

CLIFTON LAMBRETH

206

Advertorial

Continuing . . .

Jim was proud to have met and began working with John and Dan Deery at the outset and many other early automotive dealer friends where he learned an enormous amount from those days leading up to when Ray Green helped Jim to be able to speak and share concepts with many other dealers at the 1986 NADA Convention in New Orleans, LA.

It was there that Jim connected with a good number of dealers throughout the country and began what would lead to working with over 3,000 car dealers and others in the USA and around the world.

Today . . .

Today, Mudd Advertising® has thousands of clients across the USA and around the world. "We Love It When You Succeed!" was put into motion by Jim Mudd Sr. and continues to be the mantra of every business decision made by the company.

The headquarters of Mudd Advertising® are centrally located in the middle of the USA, in Cedar Falls, Iowa, on a 20 acre campus overlooking the Prairie Lakes.

Mudd headquarters houses all production, research and development teams. To say Mudd is results-driven is an understatement. The advertising solutions utilized today strive to be the most innovative and technologically-advanced products available. Through online, traditional media, mobile, video and highly targeted data offerings, the overall goal is to not only reach potential customers, but drive them to take action while maximizing market share for our clients. From beginning creative strategy to measured analytic outcomes, the partnership with Mudd for clients is an all-inclusive process for success.

The Mudd Campus is home to Iowa's largest video/sound stage: Studio 1. The studio hosts post production facilities that include Mudd Signs for creating sets as well as supporting our clients with signs, banners and a full range of POP materials. Mudd's creative concepts are managed by its award-winning, results oriented media and production teams. As part of the campus culture, employees enjoy the modern Mudd Café with delicious home-style entrees and a 24/7 fully equipped fitness center with dressing rooms and showers to keep them at the top of their game in generating results for their clients.

In addition to the 20 acre headquarter campus, Mudd has its Chicago sales office at 211 West Wacker Dr., which is conveniently located across the river from The Merchandise Mart and just down the street from Trump's Tower in downtown Chicago. Additional offices are located in Bloomington, IL, and in Nashville, TN.

HYPERCASTING®

Mudd Advertising, with more than 30 years of experience, specializes in results- oriented advertising strategies. Their latest paradigm shifting tool for the new millennium is Hypercasting®, which marries traditional advertising with the power of the Internet to create a customized result-generating solution for their clients. In fact, two of the Big Three Automotive OEM's are actively utilizing Hypercasting®, as are many national clients in the automotive world. Hypercasting® has now been expanded to sports, entertainment and the higher education verticals as well.

With the explosion of advertising on the Internet in the new millennium, Mudd realized a need for a better way to harness the marketing potential of the Web for its clients. Investing over three years of development, they sought to find ways to make the online experience more personal, direct and relevant for "buy now" consumers. The crux of the problem was: how to deliver the right message to the right customer at the right time. Mudd already had world-class demographics and analytics tools at its fingertips. The task was to embed them into an inviting virtual retail environment that would make it easier for customers to make informed purchase decisions. Their solution? Hypercasting®: an entirely new way for dealers to deliver engaging retail messages by leveraging the reach of offline media with the ubiquity of online media. The results have been astounding! Mudd has a huge hit on their hands. Hypercasting® clients are experiencing sales results like never before. With this new tool they have created a paradigm shift in the way businesses advertise, and there is no stopping it.

Hypercasting® joins the world's most persuasive medium-video-with the world's biggest showroom-the Internet, where over 90% of customers are now researching their next purchases. It turns the Internet from merely a search tool into a retailing environment that rivals any store with its ability to sell your products today.

Backed by a unique arsenal of video production capabilities, interactive developers, direct mail firepower, and an award-winning creative team, Hypercasting® can deliver a solution for your business at light speed, with a pace no competitors can match.

The agility of the Hypercasting® system to analyze results, lead quality, convergence and response rates is second to none. Client case studies speak for themselves:

Hypercasting® can gain market share, move inventory, and lead your region in activity!

World Class Resources

Mudd Advertising has resources nationwide who contribute to the company, whether by serving on the board of directors, serving our government and communities, providing consulting and leadership coaching or through their long term relationships with key industry professionals. The networking with these influential business-leading experts helps Mudd stay ahead of emerging trends in technology, corporate business, and the laws and regulations affecting their clients' business.

Frank Seng - Chief Financial Officer, Mudd Advertising. Frank consistently puts forth ideas that take Mudd Advertising to new heights each and every day. His leadership helped expand Mudd's automotive vertical by fostering new partnerships on a tier one level.

Before serving in his current role, Frank spent over 40 years working at McGladrey and Pullen LLP, one of the largest providers of assurance, tax and consulting services.   Frank has applied his technical accounting skills from public accounting and combined those skills with his unique results oriented approach to working with customers, vendors, co-workers, etc. Since his arrival at Mudd, Frank has been strategically anticipating the company's future financial needs.

David Takes - President and CEO of Doerfer Corporation and a Principal in Silverado Investments, L.C., entities he co-founded in 1995. In his role with Doerfer, Mr. Takes oversees operations, finance, legal, administrative and HR functions and takes an active interest in business development and strategic planning initiatives.

Mr. Takes spent 10 years as a partner in the law firm of Swisher & Cohrt, advising clients in both the public and private sectors on various commercial matters. He is also a Certified Public Accountant, having earned that designation in 1982.

Mr. Takes serves on the Foundation Board of the University of Northern Iowa and chairs its Technology Transfer

Section. He completed his undergraduate at the University of Northern Iowa and obtained his law degree with distinction from the University of Iowa.

Mr. Takes is currently a Mudd Advertising Board Member and he continues to assist and counsel the company in Mudd Advertising's growth and development.

<u>Greg Bunch</u> - President, Masterplan International Corp., Adjunct Professor, University of Chicago Booth School of Business.

Greg Bunch brings years of practical experience as a general manager and entrepreneur to his classes. He is the founder and president of Masterplan International Corporation, founded to help people lead wisely and well.

He works with Fortune 50, family and start-up businesses in the areas of innovation and strategy. He was also a partner at Brandtrust, a brand strategy consultancy.

Some of the companies he has worked with include American Express, Harley-Davidson, Hewlett-Packard, Kimberly-Clark and McDonald's. Mr. Bunch has served on boards and advisory boards of companies in financial services, retail, franchising and marketing.

He has been a guest lecturer teaching entrepreneurial strategy at Wheaton College. In addition, he has lectured nationally and internationally on topics related to strategy, creating customers and innovation.

Mr. Bunch earned a bachelor's degree from Wheaton College in philosophy and a master's degree in philosophy and religion from Harvard University.

Mr. Bunch brings Strategic Planning Insight and Oversight to the Mudd Advertising relationship and as a current Board Member that continues to pay dividends in the growth of Mudd Advertising and assisting the development of their clients.

Mark Rolinger – Partner Redfern, Mason, Larsen & Moore PLC. Mr. Rolinger graduated cum laude from Wartburg College and received his law degree, with distinction, from the University of Iowa. He received his

Iowa Bar admission in 1991 along with US District Court and Northern District of Iowa.

Mr. Rolinger practices primarily in the areas of business law, wills, trusts, estate planning, probate law and real estate.

His associations and memberships include Black Hawk County Bar Association, Iowa State Bar Association, Business Law, Probate and Trust Law, Real Estate and Title Law, and American Bar Association.

Mudd Advertising has utilized this law firm since its inception in 1981 and the relationship with Mr. Rolinger as a Mudd Advertising Board Member has grown over the years as he has guided the company with legal directions as it has grown and continues to grow.

Today's Client Successes . . .

. . . are a direct result of the principles enumerated throughout the book as Mudd Advertising continues to apply the strengths and principles that were first implemented by Jim Mudd Sr. more than 30 years ago. As the next generation of the Mudd family drives the legacy forward, technology is certainly a leading force. What is clear is that the technology developed today for their customers is defined by the talent behind its creation. It's the quality of the people that has helped the company grow into what it has become today.

The culture and dedication keeps the focus on truth, integrity and passion. Just as John passed along the fundamentals of leadership to Jim, these lessons continue to be shared at the core of Mudd success. Today, Mudd serves more than 3,200 clients annually and recently became supply partners with two American OEM automotive manufacturers.

Jim Mudd Sr.'s Legacy . . .

Jim's legacy resides not only in the lessons he learned within business, but also within family. While growing the company, his wife and children played an integral part in bringing success to the clients they serve today.

<u>Jim Mudd Jr.</u> - Jim Mudd Jr. now serves as the President / CEO of the company and focuses on business revenue, public relations and marketing for the Mudd Brand.

<u>Rob Mudd</u> - Rob Mudd is President of Digital Media and is responsible for all research and development of the software proprietary tools that continue to evolve the Mudd legacy into new verticals.

<u>Mary Kay Mudd Bushonville</u> - Mary Kay Mudd Bushonville has been instrumental in extending Mudd's solutions into new verticals – Academics and Athletics. Mary Kay leads Chicago and Cedar Falls teams in the for-profit education vertical and has created a new precedent in cost per lead and convergence to enrollment for major, national for-profit education entities.

<u>Chris Mudd</u> - Chris Mudd has mastered the Mudd call force and direct marketing focus for automotive. He has dedicated passion for his division and helped grow it tenfold. The monthly campaign focus for dealerships nationwide has allowed the company to continue investing in the development of tools that allow every car dealer to prosper, from the individual dealer to the original equipment manufacturers.

Kathleen Mudd Shirk - Kathleen Mudd Shirk currently operates out of Bloomington, IL, and is focused on the Academic vertical, working with colleges and universities throughout the USA and is also a Board member.

Liz Mudd Iozzo - Liz Mudd Iozzo is present in all company decisions by serving on the Board of Directors. Liz is also an accomplished photographer who successfully manages her own creative business in Chicago. Much of the still photography in Mudd Advertising productions results from Liz's talented eye. She provides direction for the company images and also its clients' images.

The Mudd Family Legacy thrives on three things:

1. Client success
2. Immediate response
3. Speed to market

All production, creative and interactive is integrated into one team all under one roof. All teams work cohesively together toward one vision.

As the evolution of technology continues, the ultimate dedication which Jim Mudd Sr. has set forth as the legacy of Mudd Advertising will stay true, thrive and keep the company and their clients moving forward by . . .

"Asking for and expecting . . . immediate results!"

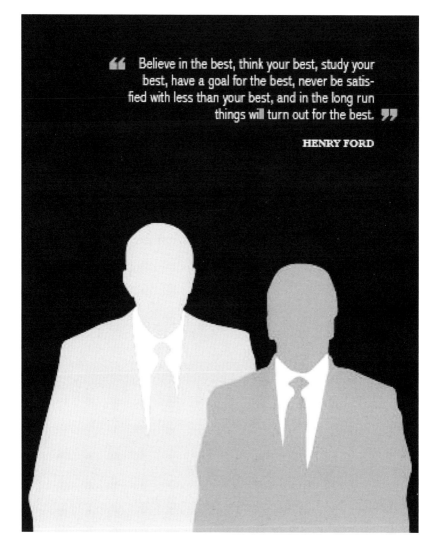

> Believe in the best, think your best, study your best, have a goal for the best, never be satisfied with less than your best, and in the long run things will turn out for the best.

HENRY FORD

Biographies

Jim Mudd Sr.

Jim Mudd Sr. serves as founder and chief spiritual officer at Mudd Advertising, and is based at the company's corporate headquarters in Cedar Falls, Iowa. He serves as chairman of the board and is responsible for consulting on the vision of the company and guiding future plans for success. As chief spiritual officer, Jim is committed to the personal and professional development of the 170 associates employed at Mudd Advertising. Jim funds a book club for associates to receive a featured book of the month focused on leadership, helping associates advance their professional careers.

Mudd Advertising opened in 1981 with just one local client and today serves thousands of automotive clients throughout the nation. The most recent additions to Mudd Advertising were a creative loft in 2010 and a state-of-the-art production studio in 2007, the largest of its kind in the state of Iowa.

Jim Mudd Sr. has helped others succeed by providing advertising advice through presentations to more than 250 different audiences. "Mudd Advertising is thankful for the many people who have helped the company grow over the past 30 years, especially our loyal clients. We are committed to providing forward-thinking advertising and marketing strategies to help our clients reach their goals."

Jim graduated from Brescia University in Owensboro, Kentucky, and attended graduate school at Northwestern University in Evanston, Illinois, focusing on radio and television broadcasting. After a respected career in broadcasting, and owning radio stations in the Midwest, he decided to create an automotive advertising agency in July of 1981. He is a national board member for the Lead Like Jesus ministry and a board member on University of Northern Iowa Foundation, and a philanthropist for many charitable organizations. Jim resides in Cedar Falls, Iowa, with his wife and business partner, Cecelia.

Clifton Peter Lambreth

Clifton Peter Lambreth is a highly sought-after business, marketing and automotive industry specialist, published author and television personality. Speaking to numerous organizations, he frequently tours the nation to present on success and business principles and has authored numerous articles on diversity, leadership, compensation and other business topics.

For over 26 years, Clifton proudly served the Ford Motor Company in a variety of positions. He was consistently a top performer throughout his career at Ford and received many prestigious awards and distinctions including five Ford Inuksuk Drive for Leaders Award, three Diversity Leadership awards, and the 2008 Ford Leadership Award.

Clifton has been a Ford college recruiter for over ten years at Cornell University, University of Pennsylvania, Johnson Business School, and Wharton Business School. He graduated from Thomasville Senior High School in North Carolina having been a proud alumnus of the North Carolina Baptist Children's Mills Home. He went on to receive his BSBA in Marketing and Management and his MBA from Western Carolina University.

Further, he is the founder and CEO of Daniel Bradley Matthews, Inc., a firm that provides strategic automotive, business and marketing consulting.

Due to his expertise and experience, Clifton has been quoted in over 400 media sources. He has done over 150 live radio show interviews and has appeared on NBC, CBS, ABC and Fox TV discussing a multitude of business topics. His first book, *Ford and the American Dream: Founded on Right Decisions*, has been translated into Russian.

Clifton serves on the Board of Directors of the Family Foundation Fun; on the National Advisory Board of Lead like Jesus Foundation; Western Carolina's Alumni Board; and on the Advisory Board for Western Carolina University's School of Business. Clifton resides in Brentwood, Tennessee.

" Be ready when opportunity comes. Luck is the time when preparation and opportunity meet. "

ROY D. CHAPLIN, JR.

To get your very own . . .

Many familiar with the Ad Man story have requested "S" Rings, pins and signage for their organizations as a way to recognize achievement for their own employees. Others want to recognize understanding and implementation of their company's values / goals and objectives. To create the tradition within your own organization, we have included the information on the following page for your convenience.

Additionally, Mudd Signs has specialized complete support packages with banners, toppers, posters, gold-type certificates of achievement and more to assist you in your company's own development programs.

For more details call Mudd Signs at: 877.637.3305 or visit Mudd Signs online: www.muddsigns.com

What others are saying about

<u>The Ad Man</u>

"The positive flow of organized information for having success is all through this book. In moving forward, going back to this reading will be a reminder of what's needed."

Dan Gable
Olympic Gold Medalist 1972

*   *   *

Over my forty years in the auto business, one theme has persisted: there are no shortcuts to success. The lessons found within The Ad Man are a true reflection of this and are a testament to the growth Mudd Advertising has helped my business achieve in the last five years.

David Wilson
Mega Dealer

*   *   *

"The first step toward selling more product is to start thinking right. In The Ad Man, Jim and Clifton get you to start thinking like you should. If you sell cars and don't read this book, you're nuts."

Roy H. Williams

New York Times & Wall Street Journal
Bestselling author of The Wizard of Ads trilogy

*   *   *

"I've had the privilege of knowing John Deery. John did us all a favor by advising Jim to become The Ad Man. In 1986 Jim came to work for a Ford Dealership in South Dakota where I was General Sales Manager. Along with his help we doubled our retail sales. In 1997 Jim and The Mudd Group came to Butte, Montana, to direct advertising of a Ford dealership that I had purchased. Once again we made great strides in increasing our retail sales. The Mudd's and The Mudd Group have been great business partners and true friends. This book sums it up!"

Brooks Hanna
Dealer

* * *

"Many people study and know of the principles required to win in life or in business. Jim Mudd Sr. not only knows and understands these principles; but he has lived them day in and out while applying them beautifully over the last 30 years to create an elite environment that is an absolute rarity in this world. That environment is known as Mudd Advertising. The Ad Man gives you an entertaining glimpse into this remarkable world and a company devoted to helping people to succeed."

Jed Smith

**Strength & Conditioning Coach /
Minnesota Vikings - NFL /
Minnesota Wild – NHL /
University Northern Iowa**

* * *

"Couldn't put it down – reminded me that after 60 years in marketing and advertising that I can't remember all that I know!"

Ike Leighty
Marketing Executive

*   *   *

Jim Mudd Sr. has built an elite advertising company by inspiring people to achieve levels of high performance.   His relentless energy and compassion for others is demonstrated throughout his company.   Mudd Advertising reflects Jim's desire to help others succeed.

Mark Farley
Head Football Coach University Northern Iowa

*   *   *

I really enjoyed the AD MAN. The book reinforces the SIMPLE TRUTH! No matter how much technology changes some principles will always remain steadfast. It's the significant principles that differentiate Jim Mudd Sr and the entire Mudd group from the INDUSTRY.

Sam Sweeden
Automotive "Imagineer"- Mudd Client since 1986

* * *

Jim Mudd and Clifton Lambreth capture and share the essence of success in business with their amazing true story of the establishment of Mudd Advertising. The meaning of the "S" ring unfolds as individual and team leadership traits are discovered and explored chapter by chapter. To learn their philosophy is to understand the principles of serving, sharing, and responding to the needs of others. I highly recommend "The Ad Man" - a compilation of positive attitudes and thoughts expressed in an easy to read and understand "life messages."

Bob Tomes
Bob Tomes Ford, McKinney, Texas

* * *

"The Ad Man" is packed with great success tips and lessons. This book reminds the reader of

time tested truths that can help improve anyone who reads it. This book also helps the reader to understand the American automotive dealer is a great environment for learning many of life's lessons. I think any business person will enjoy this book and I highly recommend it to every automotive dealer. It made me proud to be an automotive dealer.

Tony Pack

Vice President of Sam Pack Automotive Group
Author of the book "Mended By God"

*   *   *

The Ad Man book provides a great reminder that listening to your prospects and clients is the fastest way to improve your business while learning. The book is very timely as it provides a great strategy for reinventing yourself and your business as your business environment continues to change.

Brian Sykora
Sykora Family Ford, West, Texas

* * *

The Ad Man book is a great story of how to go from surviving to thriving by focusing on the right things. This book is packed with best practices and inspiration that would benefit anyone attempting to grow their business. The authors' story telling is a very effective way to share time tested principles.

Robert McGraw
AER Corporation, Carrollton, Texas

* * *

The Ad Man book does a great job of providing a roadmap to success. The story is compelling and the lessons outlined in this book will help any organization become better at whatever industry they are competing in. This book provides inspiration and education to everyone that reads it. It reminds us all that we should be on a path of continuous learning to lead any industry.

Randall Reed
World Class Automotive

*   *   *

The Ad Man book is the best collection of inspirational ideas, stories and principles that I have read in a long time! I found myself identifying with the challenges of the main character as he went from barley surviving to thriving. It is a great reminder of the power of being positive and surrounding yourself with positive people. This book is packed with quotations and stories that will inspire anyone who reads it! I recommend that not only you get a copy but get a copy for all your key managers.

Jeff Goodwin
Prestige Marketing